SRa PHONICS 1

Alvin Granowsky, Ed.D.

CONTRIBUTING AUTHORS

Joy Ann Tweedt, classroom teacher

Norman Najimy, educational consultant

REVIEWERS

Dr. Helen Brown
Director of Elementary Programs, K-8
Metropolitan Public Schools
Nashville, Tennessee

Nora Forester
Associate Superintendent for Curriculum
Archdiocese of San Antonio and
Diocese of Victoria
San Antonio, Texas

Pamela K. Francis
Principal
Seltice Elementary School
Post Falls, Idaho

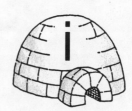

SRA

Contents

Pretests		Unit 1		Unit 2		Unit 3	
Visual Discrimination	v	**Letters of the Alphabet**	1	**Consonant Sounds**	41	**Short Vowels**	102
Visual discrimination of shapes	v	Aa, Bb, Cc, Dd	1	d, m, s	41	Short a	102
Visual discrimination of letter shapes	vi	Ee, Ff, Gg, Hh	7	b, g, t	49	Short i	113
		Ii, Jj, Kk, Ll	13	f, l, n	59	Short o	124
		Mm, Nn, Oo, Pp	19	k, p, r	67	Short e	135
		Qq, Rr, Ss, Tt	25	h, j, w	77	Short u	146
		Uu, Vv, Ww, Xx	31	c, v, y	84		
		Yy, Zz	37	qu, z, x	93		
		Unit test	40	Unit test	101	Unit test	158

CREDITS

Project Supervisor: Deborah Akers
Production Design and Development: PAT CUSICK
and ASSOCIATES
Design Director: LESIAK/CRAMPTON DESIGN INC.

ISBN 002-686009-0

13 14 15 16 17 18 19 20   DBH   07 06 05 04 03 02

Unit 4		Unit 5		Unit 6		Unit 7		Unit 8	
Long Vowels	159	**Consonant Blends**	225	**Sounds of y**	245	**Consonant Digraphs**	249	**Word Structure**	258
Long **a**	159	Blends with **s**	225	y = y, y = ē		sh	249	Plurals:	
Long **i**	173	Blends with **l**	231	y = ī	245			**-s, -es**	258
Long **o**	185	Blends with **r**	237			th	250	Inflected endings:	
Long **e**	198					ch	251	**-ed**, **-ing**	262
Long **u**	211					wh	252		
Unit test	224	Unit test	244	Unit test	248	Unit test	257	Unit test	266

l t  m

Aa

Circle each capital **A** and small **a** below.

Ⓐ K A A Y H A E F A B V

ⓐ c a o p a a b a u d a a

Circle each capital **A** and small **a** in the words below.

ⓐn day Alan make as than

Trace and then print the capital **A** and the small **a**.

A A

a a

1 Say each picture name. **2** Trace the small **a** in each word.

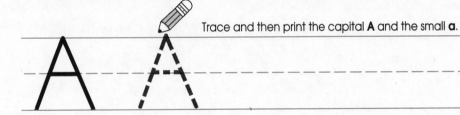

ant man ax hat

Circle each capital **B** and small **b** below.

B D R B B S B E B F B J

b p b d l b g y b d c p

Circle each capital **B** and small **b** in the words below.

be Beth big about by bed

Trace and then print the capital **B** and the small **b**.

B B

b b

1 Say each picture name. **2** Trace the small **b** in each word.

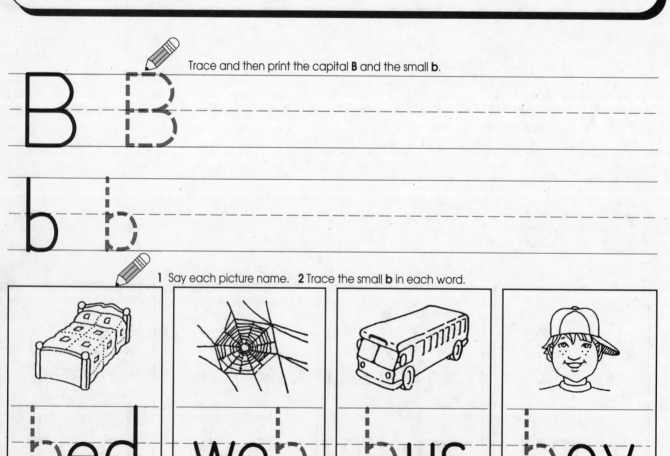

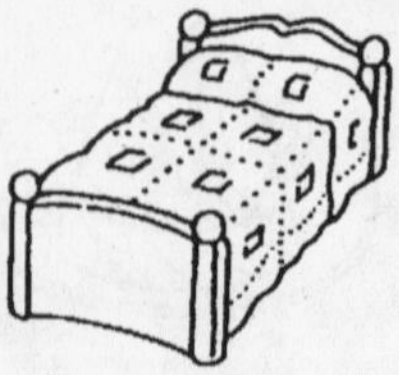			
bed	web	bus	boy

Cc

Circle each capital **C** and small **c** below.

C O C G D C C E C B J C

c a c o e c n c u c r v

Circle each capital **C** and small **c** in the words below.

cow call Coby black cold can

Trace and then print the capital **C** and the small **c**.

C C

c c

1 Say each picture name. 2 Trace the small **c** in each word.

  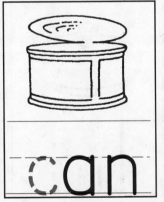 

cat cup can cap

Dd

✏ Circle each capital **D** and small **d** below.

D B O D P D R C D D A G

d a d p d d b c d o d p

✏ Circle each capital **D** and small **d** in the words below.

do down Don word did rod

✏ Trace and then print the capital **D** and the small **d**.

D D

d d

✏ **1** Say each picture name. **2** Trace the small **d** in each word.

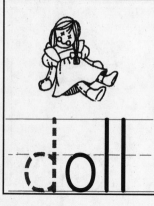

doll

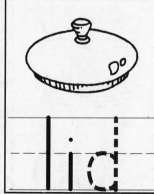

lid

bed

dog

4

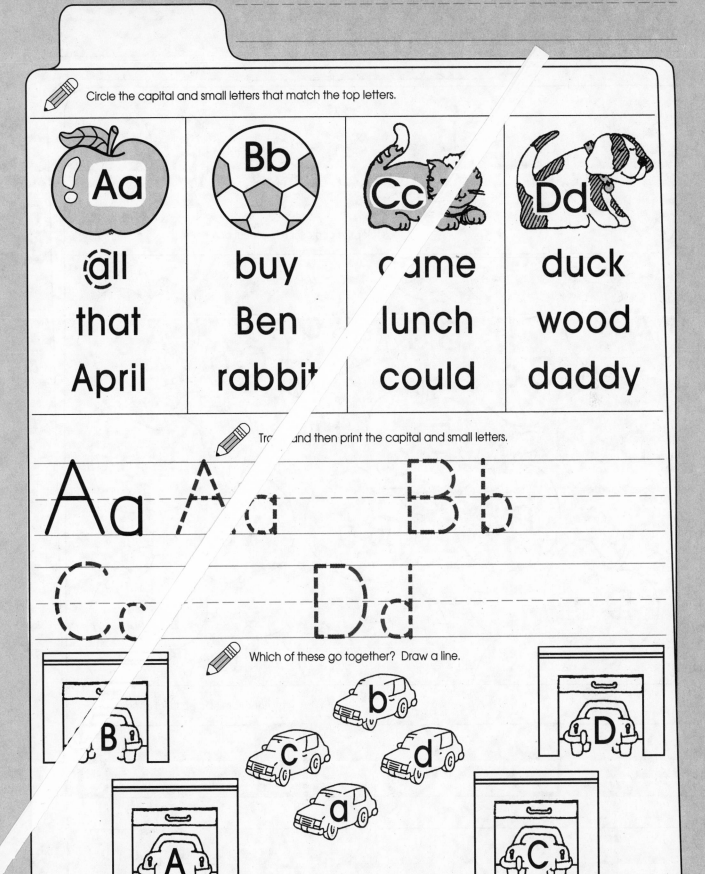

Circle the capital and small letters that match the top letters.

Aa	Bb	Cc	Dd
all	buy	came	duck
that	Ben	lunch	wood
April	rabbit	could	daddy

Trace and then print the capital and small letters.

Aa Aa   Bb

Cc   Dd

Which of these go together? Draw a line.

b
B   c
    d   D
    a
A   C

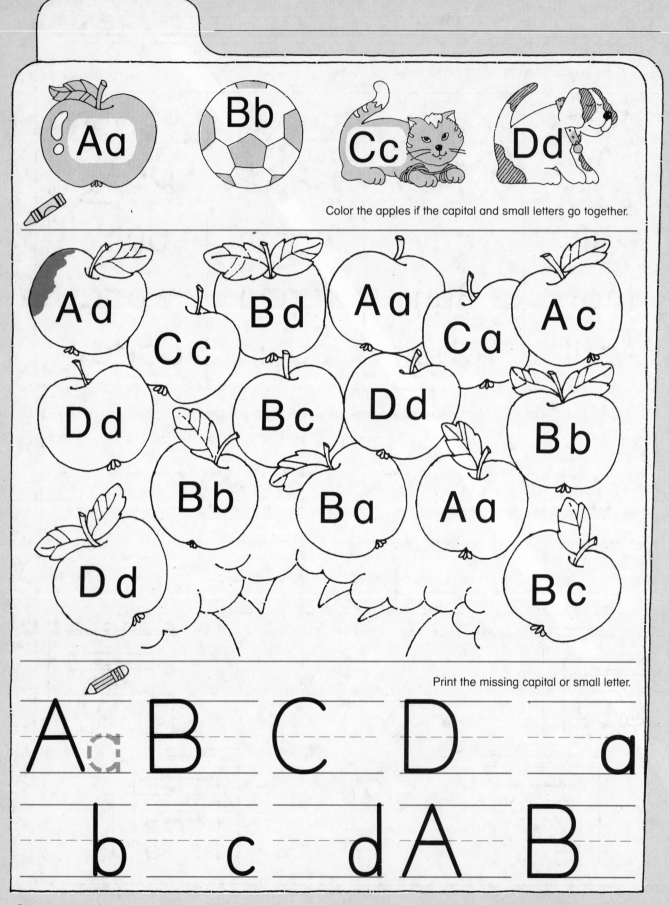

Aa   Bb   Cc   Dd

Color the apples if the capital and small letters go together.

Aa   Bd   Aa   Ac
  Cc   Ca
Dd   Bc   Dd   Bb
  Bb   Ba   Aa
Dd   Bc

Print the missing capital or small letter.

A B C D a

b c d A B

Reviewing the letters of the alphabet; **Aa**, **Bb**, **Cc**, **Dd**

Ee

Circle each capital **E** and small **e** below.

Ⓔ R B M E H E S L E Z E
ⓔ s o e c e n e a u e c

Circle each capital **E** and small **e** in the words below.

s ⓔⓔ eat Eve like Steve she

Trace and then print the capital **E** and the small **e**.

E E̲

e e̲

1 Say each picture name. **2** Trace the small **e** in each word.

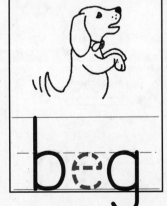

leg wet beg hen

Introducing the letters of the alphabet; **Ee**

7

Ff

Circle each capital **F** and small **f** below.

Ⓕ P E F F K B F V F Y F

ⓕ k b h f t f h d f f p

Circle each capital **F** and small **f** in the words below.

ⓕur from Friday fun before off

Trace and then print the capital **F** and the small **f**.

F

f

1 Say each picture name. 2 Trace the small **f** in each word.

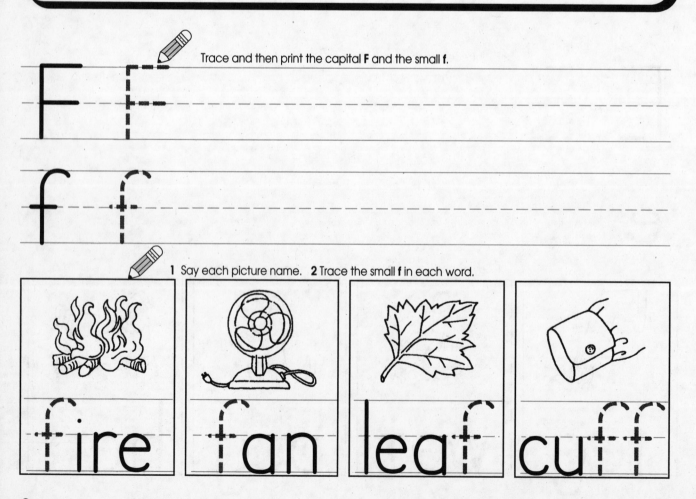

fire   fan   leaf   cuff

Introducing the letters of the alphabet; **Ff**

G g

Circle each capital **G** and small **g** below.

(G) C P G D G G J G Q U G

(g) b y g g j g p d g q g

Circle each capital **G** and small **g** in the words below.

(g)o hug Glen give snug bag

Trace and then print the capital **G** and the small **g**.

G G

g g

1 Say each picture name. 2 Trace the small **g** in each word.

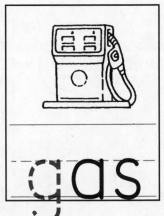

girl pig bug gas

Introducing the letters of the alphabet; **Gg**

9

Hh

Circle each capital **H** and small **h** below.

(H) B K I H E H H F H H M

(h) d h k b h n f h h l h

Circle each capital **H** and small **h** in the words below.

(h)im hold ship Hope who this

Trace and then print the capital **H** and the small **h**.

H H

h h

1 Say each picture name. **2** Trace the small **h** in each word.

hat

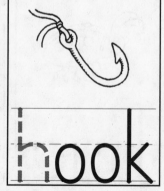
hook

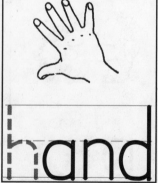
hand

horn

10

Circle the capital and small letters that match the top letters.

Ee

feet

Ellen

these

Ff

farm

fluffy

Florida

Gg

bag

garden

rug

Hh

hand

Hannah

which

Trace and then print the capital and small letters.

E e E e

F f

G g

H h

Which of these go together? Draw a line.

F

g

f

h

e

H

G

E

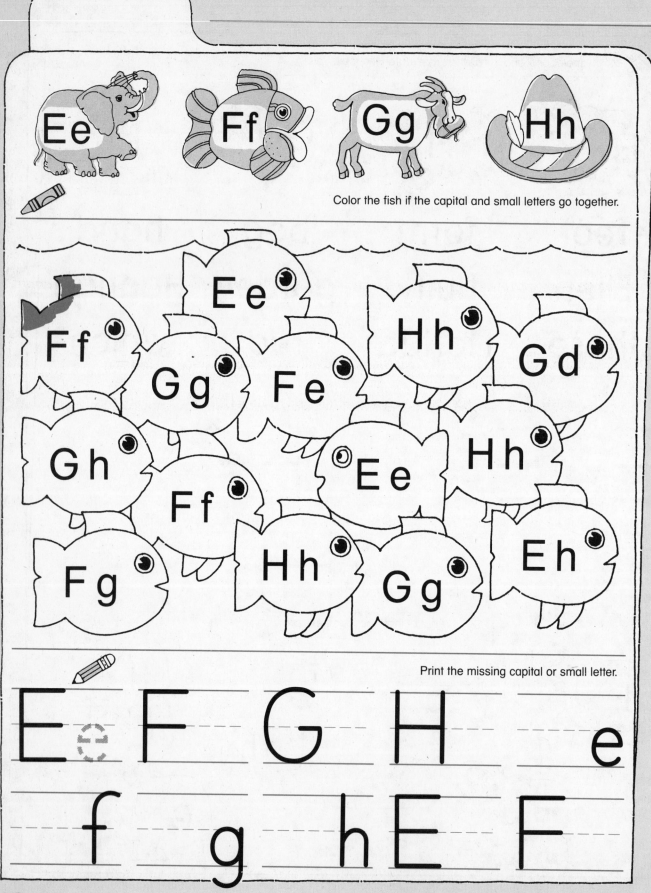

Ee   Ff   Gg   Hh

Color the fish if the capital and small letters go together.

Ff   Ee   Fe   Hh   Gd

Gg

Gh   Ee   Hh

Ff

Fg   Hh   Gg   Eh

Print the missing capital or small letter.

E F G H   e

f   g h E F

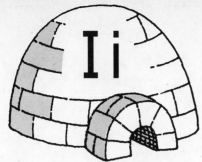

I i

Circle each capital **I** and small **i** below.

I E L I I J T I H I F

i j l i t i v r i i h

Circle each capital **I** and small **i** in the words below.

in Ivan time with into write

Trace and then print the capital **I** and the small **i**.

I I

i i

1 Say each picture name. 2 Trace the small **i** in each word.

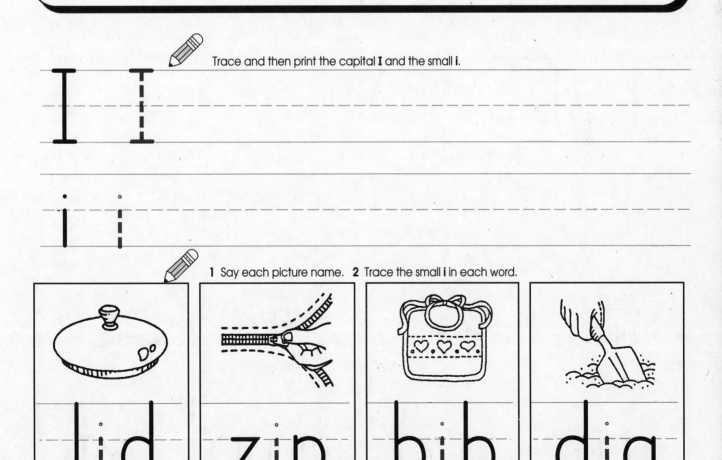

lid   zip   bib   dig

Jj

Circle each capital **J** and small **j** below.

(J) F I U J J S J G T J P

(j) i j l y j j i j u i j

Circle each capital **J** and small **j** in the words below.

(j)ust Joy junk jet join pajamas

Trace and then print the capital **J** and the small **j**.

J J

j j

1 Say each picture name. **2** Trace the small **j** in each word.

 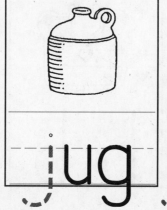  

jar jug jump jet

14

K k

Circle each capital **K** and small **k** below.

(K) E K P F K B K H K K R

(k) h r n k k f k t k k s

Circle each capital **K** and small **k** in the words below.

loo(k) Karen kitten basket park

Trace and then print the capital **K** and the small **k**.

K K

k k

1 Say each picture name. **2** Trace the small **k** in each word.

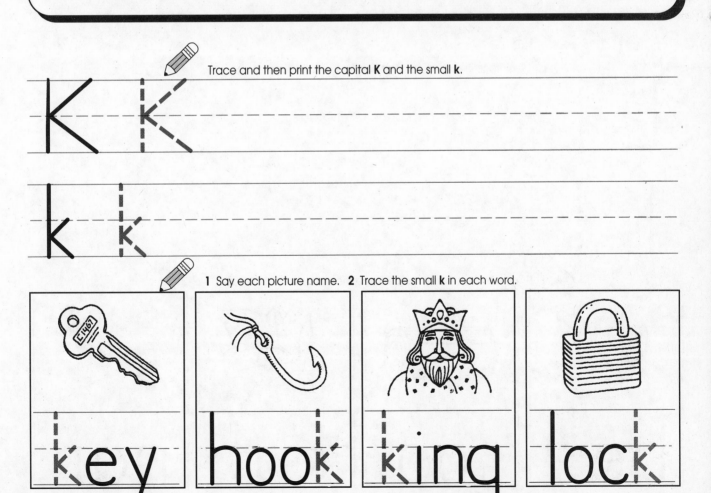

key hook king lock

Introducing the letters of the alphabet; **Kk**

15

Ll

Circle each capital **L** and small **l** below.

(L) E I U L F L V L J L

(l) f i l l h l t l i k

Circle each capital **L** and small **l** in the words below.

hi(ll)   little   hello   Lucy   July

Trace and then print the capital **L** and the small **l**.

L

l

1 Say each picture name.   **2** Trace the small **l** in each word.

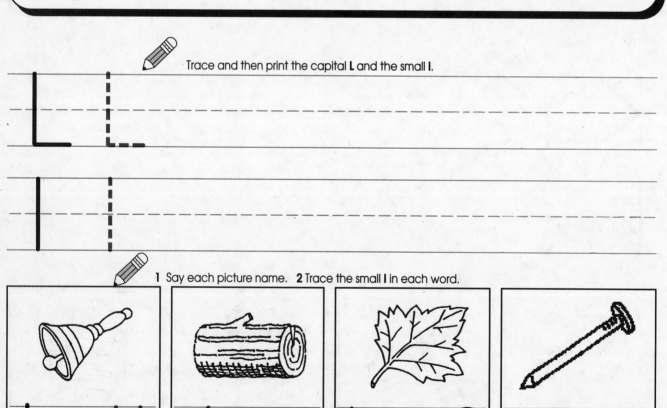

bell   log   leaf   nail

16

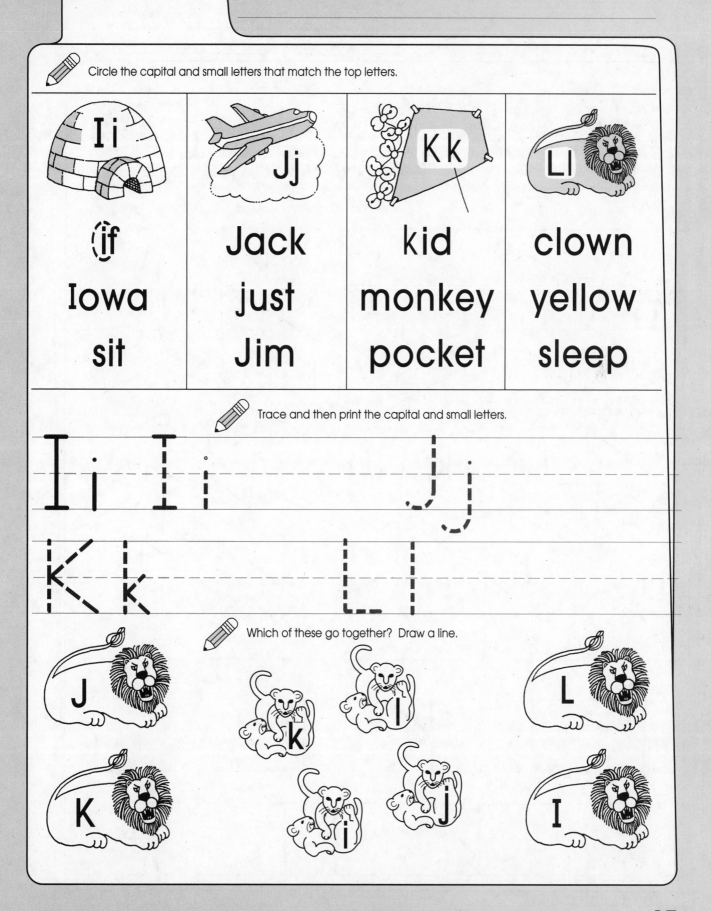

Circle the capital and small letters that match the top letters.

I i

if
Iowa
sit

J j

Jack
just
Jim

K k

kid
monkey
pocket

L l

clown
yellow
sleep

Trace and then print the capital and small letters.

I i I i

J j

K k

L l

Which of these go together? Draw a line.

J

K

k

l

i

j

L

I

Color the kites if the capital and small letters go together.

Print the missing capital or small letter.

I   J   K   L   i

    j   k   l   J

Reviewing the letters of the alphabet; **Ii, Jj, Kk, Ll**

Mm

Circle each capital **M** and small **m** below.

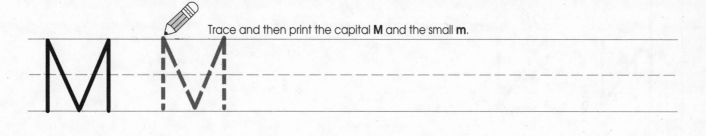

M N M V Y M E M R M M W

m n m o u m e m r m m s

Circle each capital **M** and small **m** in the words below.

them my Mary animal some

Trace and then print the capital **M** and the small **m**.

M M

m m

1 Say each picture name. 2 Trace the small **m** in each word.

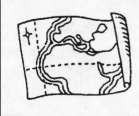 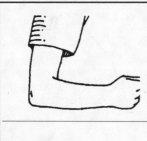 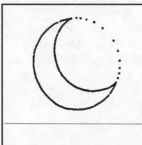 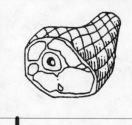

map   arm   moon   ham

Nn

Circle each capital **N** and small **n** below.

(N) H N M E N K N X N S N

(n) n c r n m n h u n o n

Circle each capital **N** and small **n** in the words below.

any one not then now Nancy

Trace and then print the capital **N** and the small **n**.

N N

n n

1 Say each picture name. 2 Trace the small **n** in each word.

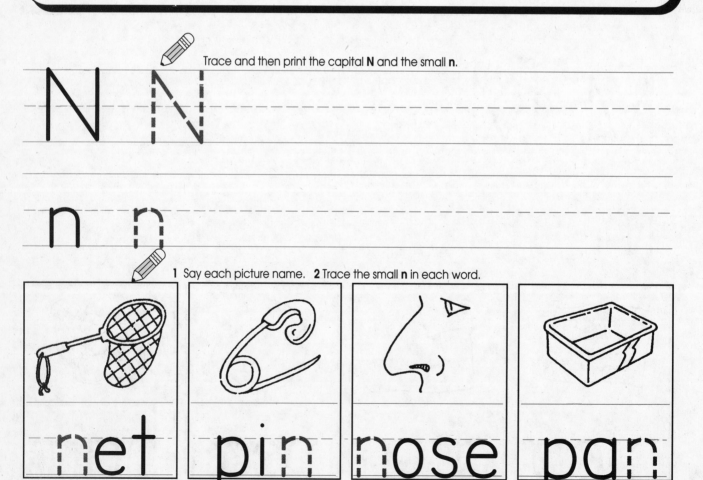

net   pin   nose   pan

Oo

✏ Circle each capital **O** and small **o** below.

Ⓞ C D O P O U G O Q O O

Ⓞ c u o a o e o e o n

✏ Circle each capital **O** and small **o** in the words below.

gⓞ Otto bone so coat float

✏ Trace and then print the capital **O** and the small **o**.

O O⃝

o o⃝

✏ **1** Say each picture name. **2** Trace the small **o** in each word.

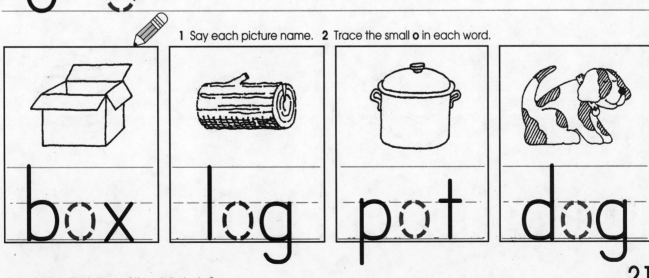

box   log   pot   dog

Pp

✏️ Circle each capital **P** and small **p** below.

(P) P D F P B P K T P R P E

(p) d h p y g p b p p q p

✏️ Circle each capital **P** and small **p** in the words below.

(p)ull stop Pam peanut puppy pig

✏️ Trace and then print the capital **P** and the small **p**.

P P

p p

✏️ **1** Say each picture name.   **2** Trace the small **p** in each word.

mop   pan   pig   top

Circle the capital and small letters that match the top letters.

 Mm	 Nn	 Oo	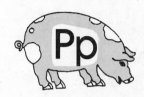 Pp
Meg	hen	old	pet
game	sand	Owen	step
Monday	barn	cold	Parker

 Trace and then print the capital and small letters.

 Mm Mm Nn

Oo Pp

 N

 M

 Which of these go together? Draw a line.

 m

 n

 o

 p

 P

 O

Reviewing the letters of the alphabet; **Mm, Nn, Oo, Pp**

Mm Nn Oo Pp

Color the pigs if the capital and small letters go together.

Pp Pb Nn

Oo Mk Nk Oo

Oo Nn

Mm Pp Nm Po

Print the missing capital or small letter.

M m N O P m

n o p M N

Reviewing the letters of the alphabet; **Mm, Nn, Oo, Pp**

Circle each capital **Q** and small **q** below.

Q O U D Q G C Q O Q C Q

q d j q g p q g q y p q

Circle each capital **Q** and small **q** in the words below.

queen quack quick Iraq Quinn

Trace and then print the capital **Q** and the small **q**.

Q Q

q q

1 Say each picture name. **2** Trace the small **q** in each word.

queen

quiet

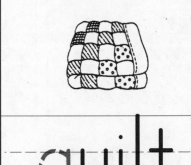

quilt

Introducing the letters of the alphabet; **Qq**

25

R r

Circle each capital **R** and small **r** below.

(R) B H R D R K E R F R P

(r) n c x r n r u z r u r

Circle each capital **R** and small **r** in the words below.

(R)oberta her rain Murray first

Trace and then print the capital **R** and the small **r**.

R R

r r

1 Say each picture name. **2** Trace the small **r** in each word.

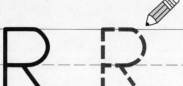

rain   ear    rug    four

26

Introducing the letters of the alphabet; **Rr**

Ss

✏ Circle each capital **S** and small **s** below.

Ⓢ K N S S B G S E S S C

Ⓢ r e s k s s x u s c s

✏ Circle each capital **S** and small **s** in the words below.

aṣk Sue super dress last bus

✏ Trace and then print the capital **S** and the small **s**.

S S̷

s s̷

✏ **1** Say each picture name. **2** Trace the small **s** in each word.

six

bus̷

saw

gas̷

Introducing the letters of the alphabet; **Ss**

Tt

Circle each capital **T** and small **t** below.

(T) Y K J T E T T H T L T

(t) t k d t l t t b f r t

Circle each capital **T** and small **t** in the words below.

better catch Tom hat went train

Trace and then print the capital **T** and the small **t**.

T T

t t

1 Say each picture name. **2** Trace the small **t** in each word.

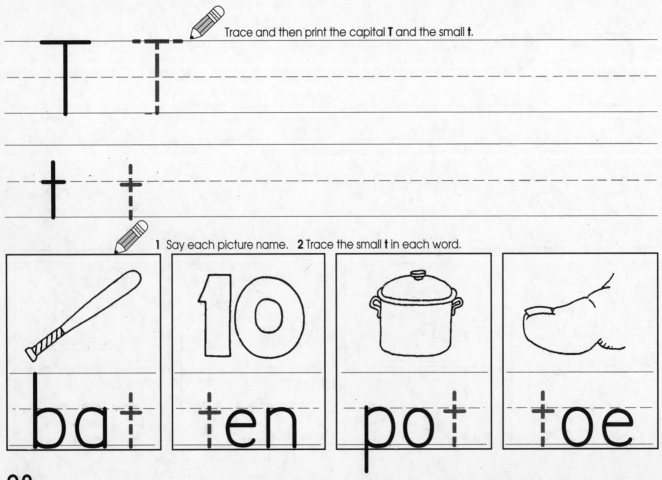

bat   ten   pot   toe

Introducing the letters of the alphabet; **Tt**

Circle the capital and small letters that match the top letters.

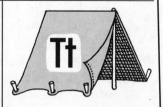

(q)uiet	hurry	sunset	Terry
Quincy	reader	Susan	time
quail	car	nose	turtle

Trace and then print the capital and small letters.

Qq   Qq   Rr

Ss   Tt

Which of these go together? Draw a line.

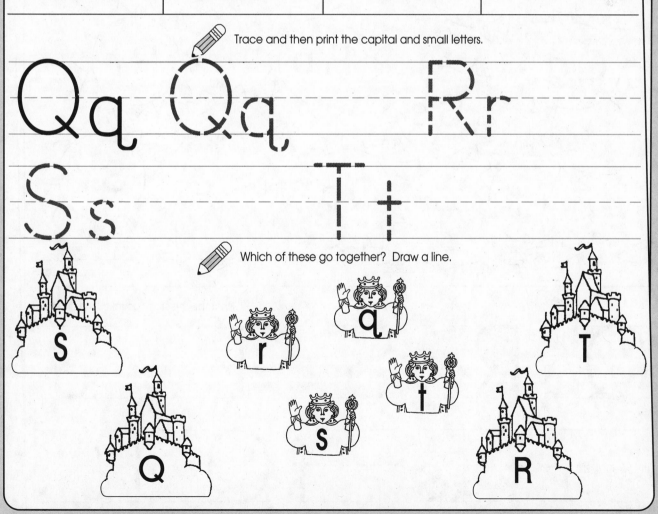

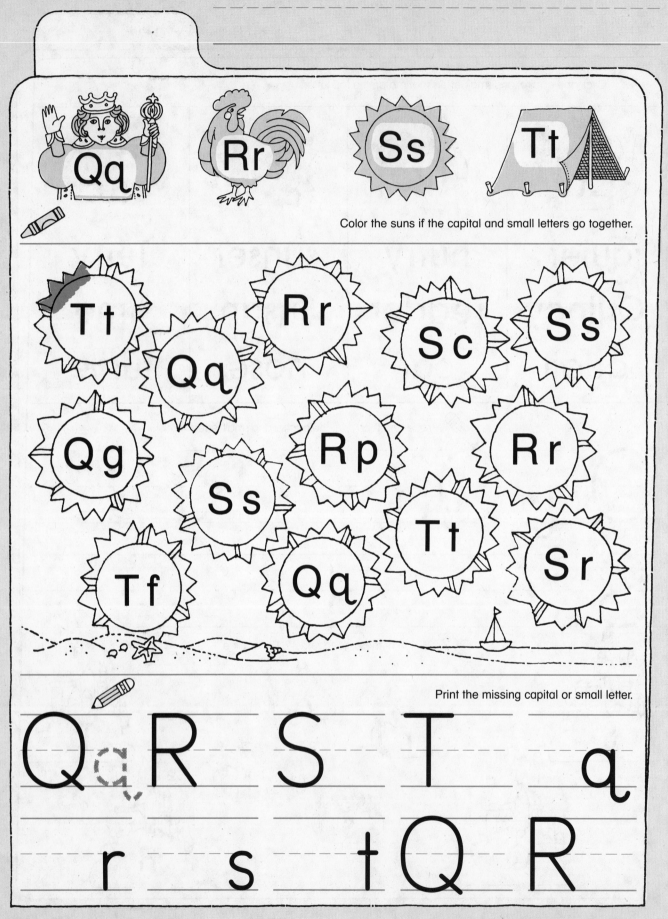

Qq   Rr   Ss   Tt

Color the suns if the capital and small letters go together.

Print the missing capital or small letter.

Q R S T q

r s t Q R

Reviewing the letters of the alphabet; **Qq**, **Rr**, **Ss**, **Tt**

Uu

Circle each capital **U** and small **u** below.

U D O J U U V U N C U Y

u n u v r u h c u n v u

Circle each capital **U** and small **u** in the words below.

use cube fun U.S.A. much up

Trace and then print the capital **U** and the small **u**.

U U

u u

1 Say each picture name.　**2** Trace the small **u** in each word.

  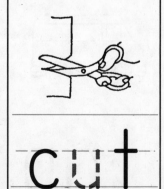 

nut　bug　cut　run

Vv

Circle each capital **V** and small **v** below.

Ⓥ N Z V W V M X V Y K V

ⓥ r w u v x v y k v v n

Circle each capital **V** and small **v** in the words below.

haⓥe cave over Virginia visit

Trace and then print the capital **V** and the small **v**.

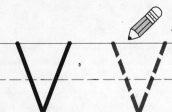

V V

V V

1 Say each picture name. 2 Trace the small **v** in each word.

vest van vase vine

32

Circle each capital **W** and small **w** below.

Ⓦ M V E W K W N Y W Z W

Ⓦ m v w x w m z w v w m

Circle each capital **W** and small **w** in the words below.

Ⓦ**ayne brown forward will grew**

Trace and then print the capital **W** and the small **w**.

W W

W W

1 Say each picture name. **2** Trace the small **w** in each word.

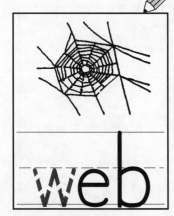

web

wave

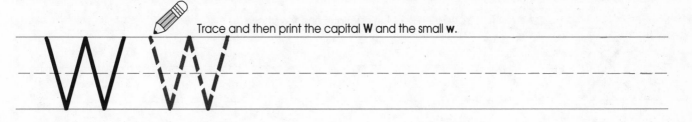

wing

well

Introducing the letters of the alphabet; **Ww**

Xx

Circle each capital **X** and small **x** below.

Ⓧ X X K Y H E X X W Z X V

ⓧ r t z X z w X X u v r x

Circle each small **x** in the words below.

ⓧ-ray mix tax exit box ax

Trace and then print the capital **X** and the small **x**.

X ⟋⟍

x ⤬

1 Say each picture name. 2 Trace the small **x** in each word.

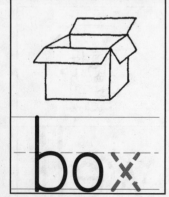

box six mix fox

Circle the capital and small letters that match the top letters.

Uu	Vv	Ww	Xx
butter	never	water	wax
Utah	very	twin	ox
until	live	away	six

Trace and then print the capital and small letters.

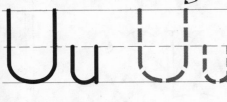

Uu Uu   Vv

Ww   Xx

Which of these go together? Draw a line.

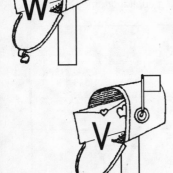

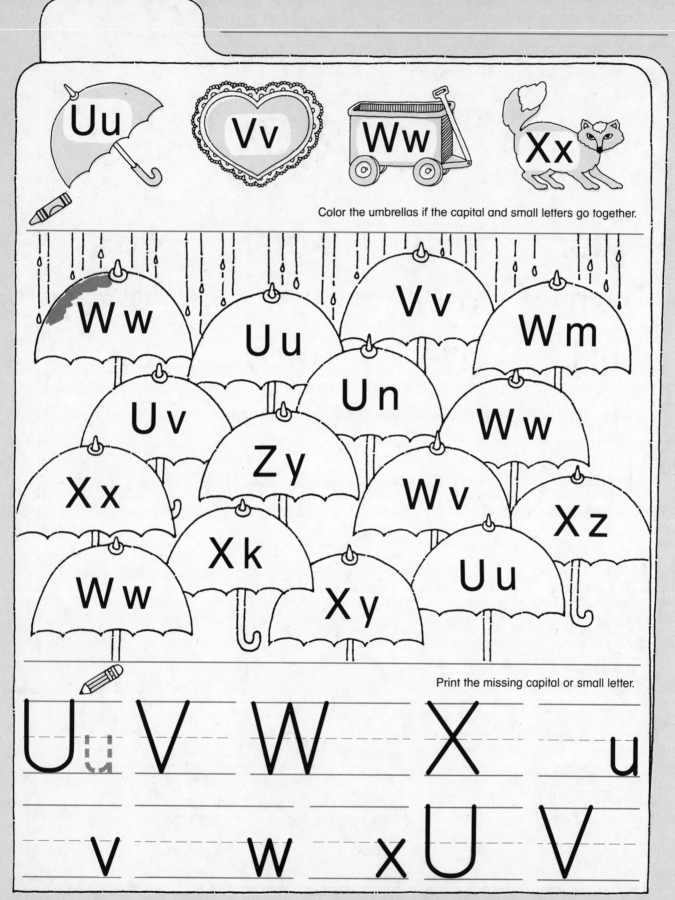

Color the umbrellas if the capital and small letters go together.

Print the missing capital or small letter.

Reviewing the letters of the alphabet; **Uu**, **Vv**, **Ww**, **Xx**

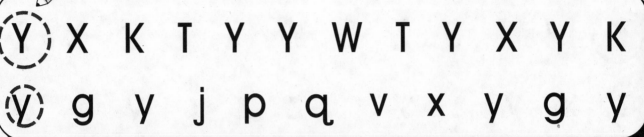

Circle each capital **Y** and small **y** below.

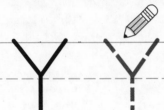

Y X K T Y Y W T Y X Y K

y g y j p q v x y g y

Circle each capital **Y** and small **y** in the words below.

day fly yellow Yolanda my pony

Trace and then print the capital **Y** and the small **y**.

Y Y

y y

1 Say each picture name. **2** Trace the small **y** in each word.

yarn

yell

yawn

yard

Z z

Circle each capital **Z** and small **z** below.

(Z) M T S Z E W Z Y Z X Z

(z) x v z s n z z s y v z

Circle each capital **Z** and small **z** in the words below.

(z)oo Zeke zero buzz zebra lazy

Trace and then print the capital **Z** and the small **z**.

Z Z

z z

1 Say each picture name. 2 Trace the small **z** in each word.

zoo zebra zero

38

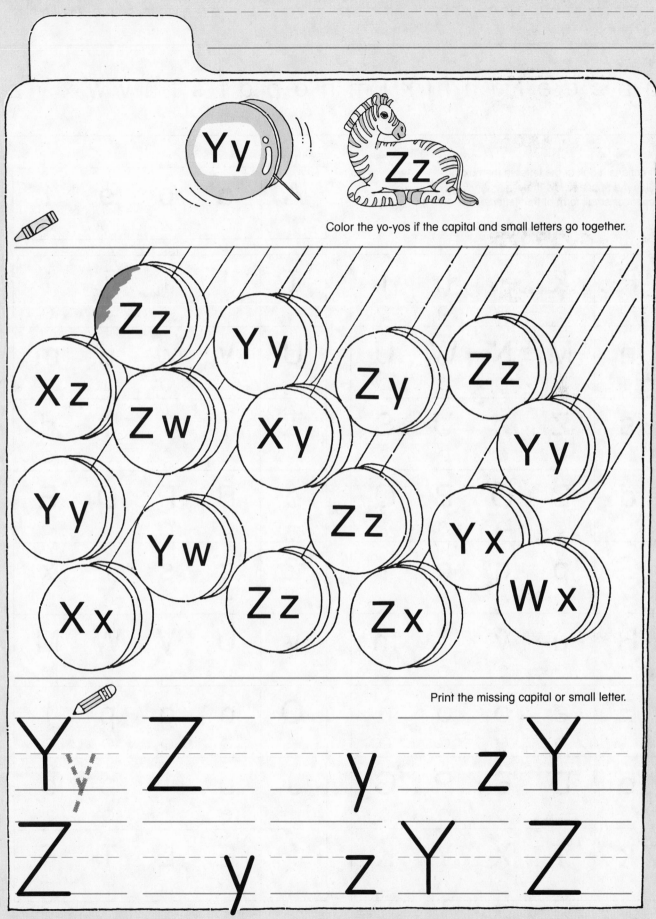

Color the yo-yos if the capital and small letters go together.

Print the missing capital or small letter.

_____

_ _

_____

a b c d e f g h i j k l m n o p q r s t u v w x y z

_____

Directions: Look at the letter in the box.
Fill in the space below the
capital or small form of that letter.

Example

A	a	o	e	i
	○	○	○	○

H	k	l	h	t
	○	○	○	○
n	M	N	W	U
	○	○	○	○
s	Z	X	U	S
	○	○	○	○
d	D	O	B	Q
	○	○	○	○
G	p	q	g	j
	○	○	○	○
R	u	v	r	m
	○	○	○	○
E	e	o	a	u
	○	○	○	○
b	D	B	P	G
	○	○	○	○
k	T	X	Y	K
	○	○	○	○

I	l	i	j	t
	○	○	○	○
U	v	w	u	m
	○	○	○	○
T	t	l	f	d
	○	○	○	○
p	B	P	D	E
	○	○	○	○
Z	z	s	r	x
	○	○	○	○
v	U	V	W	M
	○	○	○	○
Q	q	g	p	j
	○	○	○	○
J	g	j	p	q
	○	○	○	○
f	E	L	T	F
	○	○	○	○

Testing the letters of the alphabet; using an adapted standardized test format

1 Say each picture name.
2 Listen to the first sound.
3 Color the picture if its name begins with the sound of **d**.

Introducing the consonant sound of **d**

d

42

Using the consonant sound of **d** in initial and final positions

1 Say each picture name.
2 Listen to the first sound.
3 Color the picture if its name begins with the sound of **m**.

43

Introducing the consonant sound of **m**

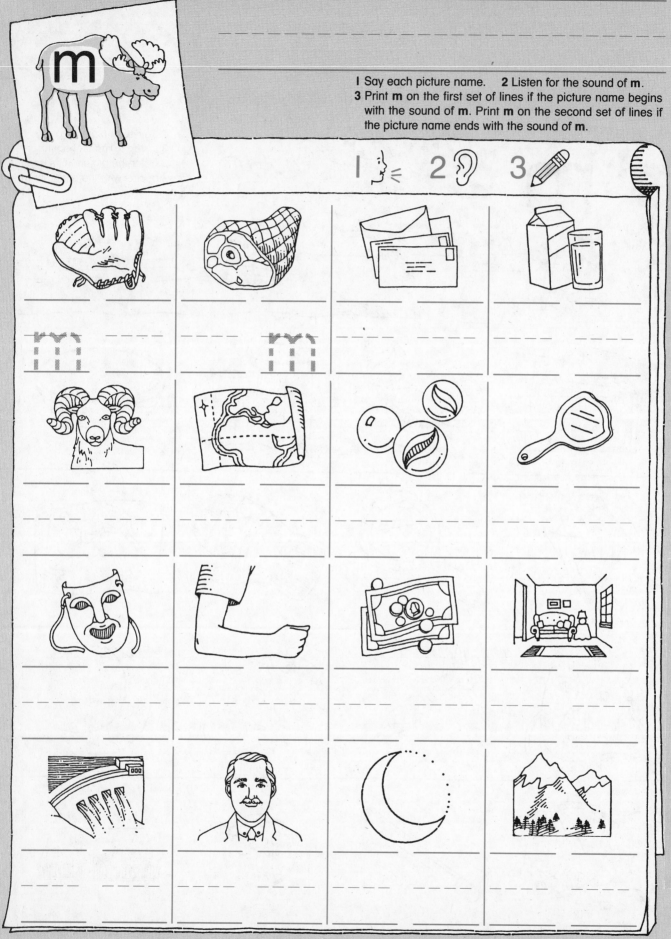

1 Say each picture name. 2 Listen for the sound of **m**.
3 Print **m** on the first set of lines if the picture name begins with the sound of **m**. Print **m** on the second set of lines if the picture name ends with the sound of **m**.

44

S

1 Say each picture name.
2 Listen to the first sound.
3 Color the picture if its name begins with the sound of **s**.

Introducing the consonant sound of **s**

1 Say each picture name. 2 Listen for the sound of **s**.
3 Print **s** on the first set of lines if the picture name begins with the sound of **s**. Print **s** on the second set of lines if the picture name ends with the sound of **s**.

1 👄 2 👂 3 ✏️

46

Using the consonant sound of **s** in initial and final positions

d m s

1 Say each picture name. 2 Listen to the first sound.
3 Color the two pictures that begin with the same sound.
4 Then print the letter that stands for their first sound.

1 2 3 4

d

Reviewing the consonant sounds of **d**, **m**, **s** in initial position

47

1 Say each picture name.
2 Listen to the last sound.
3 Print the letter that stands for that sound.

d m s

1 2 3

m

48

Reviewing the consonant sounds of **d**, **m**, **s** in final position

1 Say each picture name.
2 Listen to the first sound.
3 Color the picture if its name begins with the sound of **b**.

Introducing the consonant sound of **b**

50

Using the consonant sound of **b** in initial and final positions

g

1 Say each picture name.
2 Listen to the first sound.
3 Color the picture if its name begins with the sound of **g**.

Introducing the consonant sound of g

51

1 Say each picture name. 2 Listen for the sound of **g**.
3 Print **g** on the first set of lines if the picture name begins with the sound of **g**. Print **g** on the second set of lines if the picture name ends with the sound of **g**.

Using the consonant sound of **g** in initial and final positions

1 Say each picture name.
2 Listen to the first sound.
3 Color the picture if its name begins with the sound of t.

Introducing the consonant sound of t

53

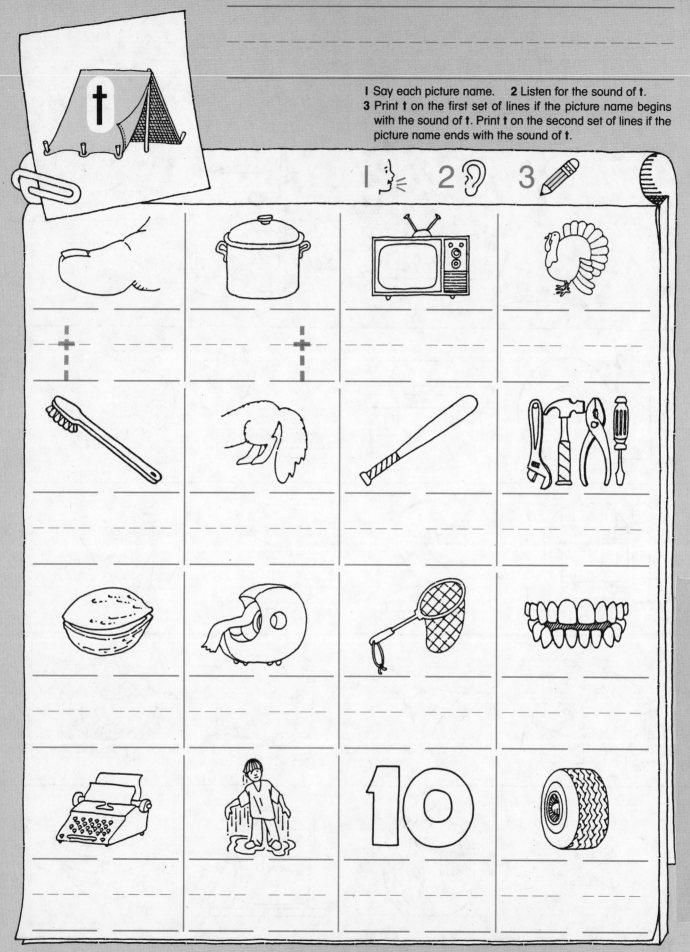

1 Say each picture name.   2 Listen for the sound of **t**.
3 Print **t** on the first set of lines if the picture name begins
   with the sound of **t**. Print **t** on the second set of lines if the
   picture name ends with the sound of **t**.

54

b   g   t

1 Say each picture name.   2 Listen to the first sound.
3 Color the two pictures that begin with the same sound.
4 Then print the letter that stands for their first sound.

1 ⤸   2 👂   3 ✏️   4 ✏️

Reviewing the consonant sounds of **b**, **g**, **t** in initial position

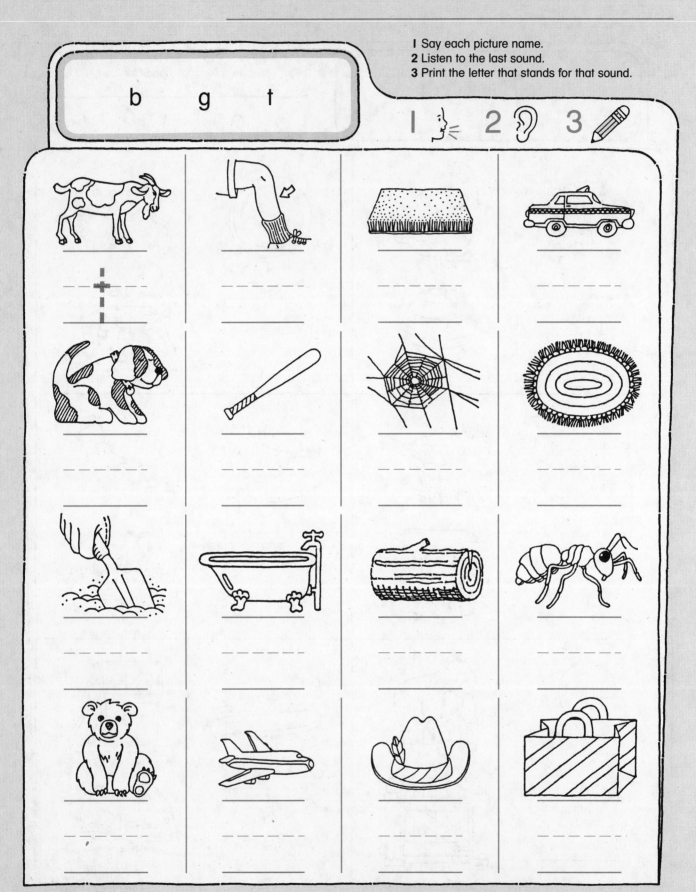

b g t

1 Say each picture name.
2 Listen to the last sound.
3 Print the letter that stands for that sound.

1 2 3

56

Reviewing the consonant sounds of **b**, **g**, **t** in final position

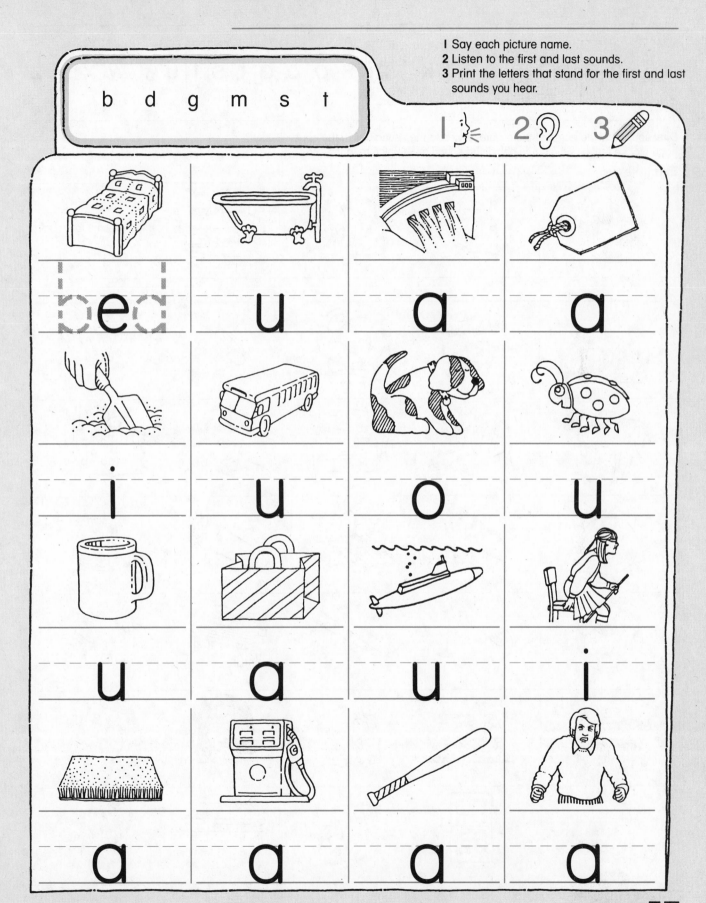

b d g m s t

1 Say each picture name.
2 Listen to the first and last sounds.
3 Print the letters that stand for the first and last sounds you hear.

bed   u   a   a

i   u   o   u

u   a   u   i

a   a   a   a

Reviewing the consonant sounds of **b**, **d**, **g**, **m**, **s**, **t** in initial and final positions a b c d e f g h i j k l m n o p q r s t u v w x y z

Directions: Say the name of the picture. Listen to the sound. Fill in the space below
each picture that has the same beginning sound as the picture in the box.

Example

Testing the consonant sounds of **b, d, g, m, s, t**; using an adapted standardized test format

f

1 Say each picture name.
2 Listen to the first sound.
3 Color the picture if its name begins with the sound of **f**.

1 Say each picture name. 2 Listen for the sound of **f**.
3 Print **f** on the first set of lines if the picture name begins
with the sound of **f**. Print **f** on the second set of lines if the
picture name ends with the sound of **f**.

60

1 Say each picture name.
2 Listen to the first sound.
3 Color the picture if its name begins with the sound of l.

1 Say each picture name. 2 Listen for the sound of l.
3 Print l on the first set of lines if the picture name begins
with the sound of l. Print l on the second set of lines if the
picture name ends with the sound of l.

62

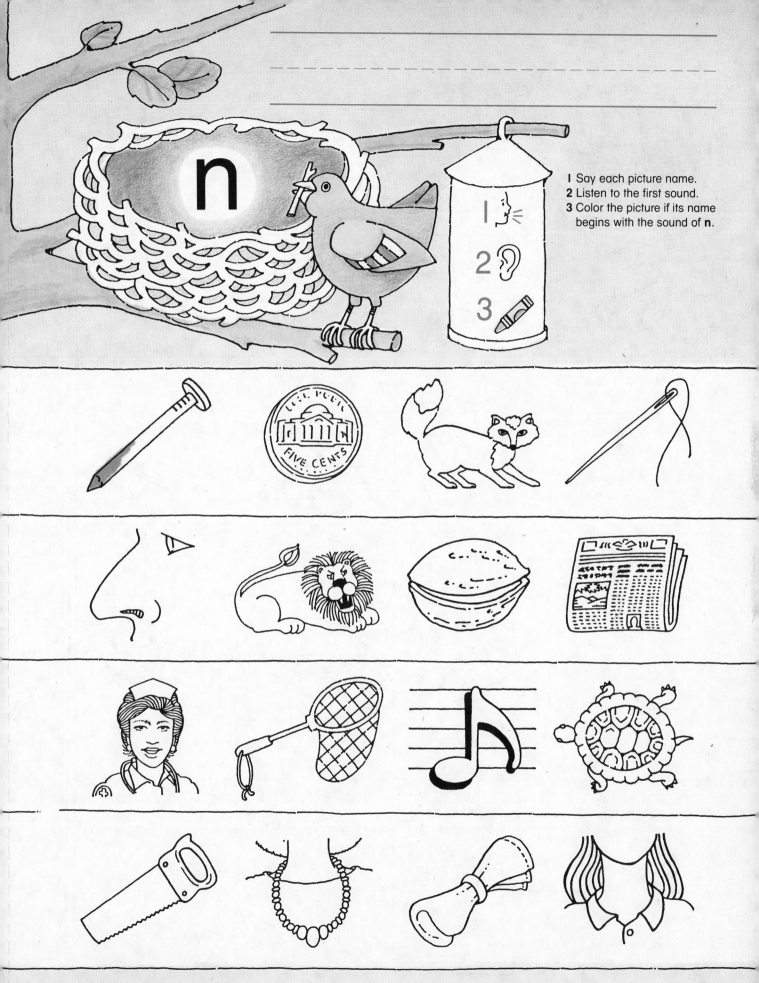

1 Say each picture name.
2 Listen to the first sound.
3 Color the picture if its name begins with the sound of **n**.

1 Say each picture name. **2** Listen for the sound of **n**.

3 Print **n** on the first set of lines if the picture name begins with the sound of **n**. Print **n** on the second set of lines if the picture name ends with the sound of **n**.

1 🗣 2 👂 3 ✏️

n   n

Using the consonant sound of **n** in initial and final positions

f l n

1 Say each picture name.   2 Listen to the first sound.
3 Color the two pictures that begin with the same sound.
4 Then print the letter that stands for their first sound.

Reviewing the consonant sounds of **f, l, n** in initial position

1 Say each picture name.
2 Listen to the last sound.
3 Print the letter that stands for that sound.

f l n

1 2 3

66

Reviewing the consonant sounds of **f, l, n** in final position

k

1 Say each picture name.
2 Listen to the first sound.
3 Color the picture if its name begins with the sound of **k**.

1 Say each picture name.   2 Listen for the sound of **k**.
3 Print **k** on the first set of lines if the picture name begins with the sound of **k**. Print **k** on the second set of lines if the picture name ends with the sound of **k**.

1 2 3

Using the consonant sound of **k** in initial and final positions

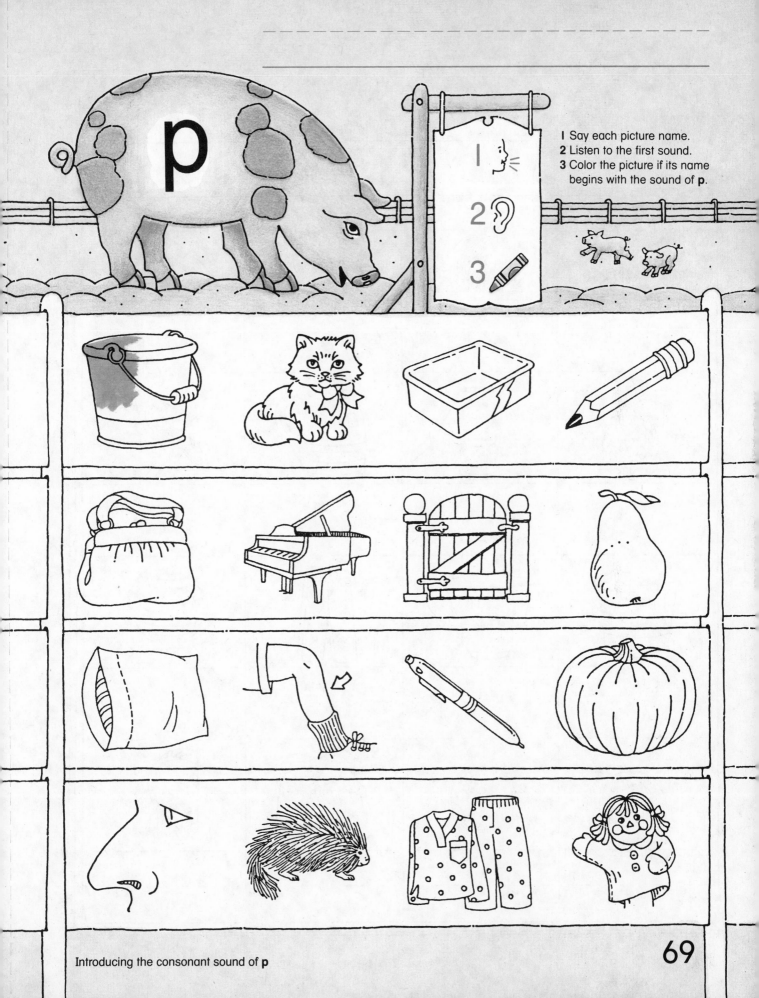

p

1 Say each picture name.
2 Listen to the first sound.
3 Color the picture if its name begins with the sound of **p**.

1 Say each picture name.   2 Listen for the sound of **p**.
3 Print **p** on the first set of lines if the picture name begins with the sound of **p**. Print **p** on the second set of lines if the picture name ends with the sound of **p**.

70

Using the consonant sound of **p** in initial and final positions

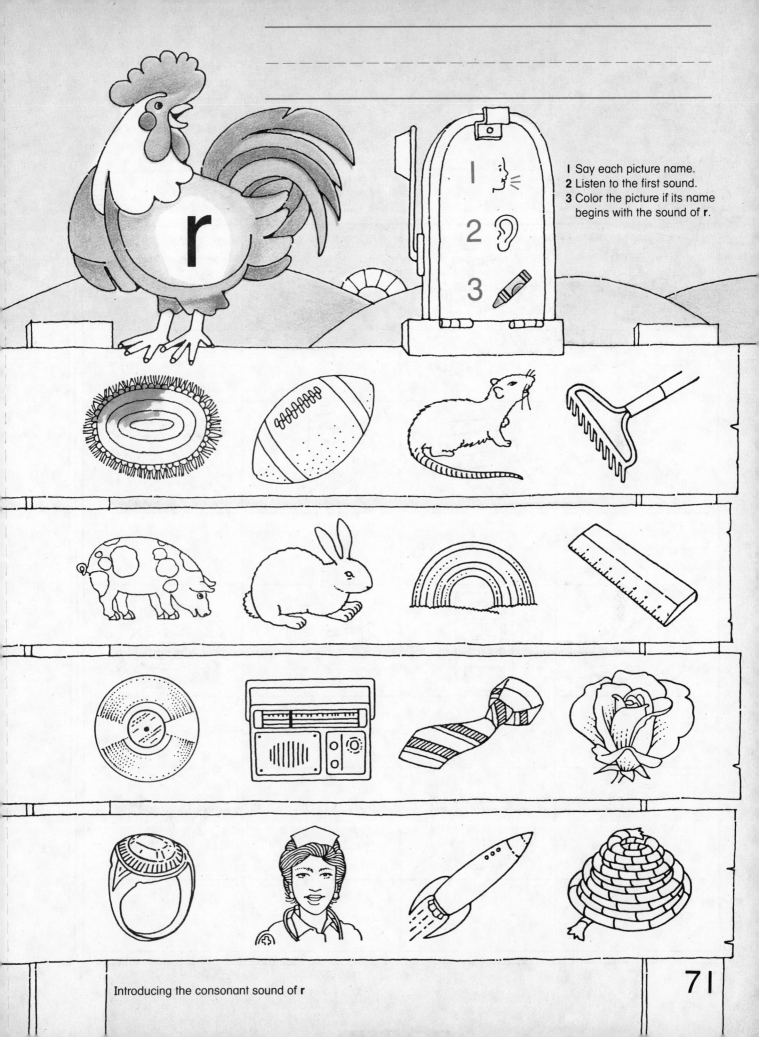

1 Say each picture name.
2 Listen to the first sound.
3 Color the picture if its name begins with the sound of **r**.

Introducing the consonant sound of **r**

72

Using the consonant sound of **r** in initial and final positions

1 Say each picture name.   2 Listen to the first sound.
3 Color the two pictures that begin with the same sound.
4 Then print the letter that stands for their first sound.

1 2 3 4

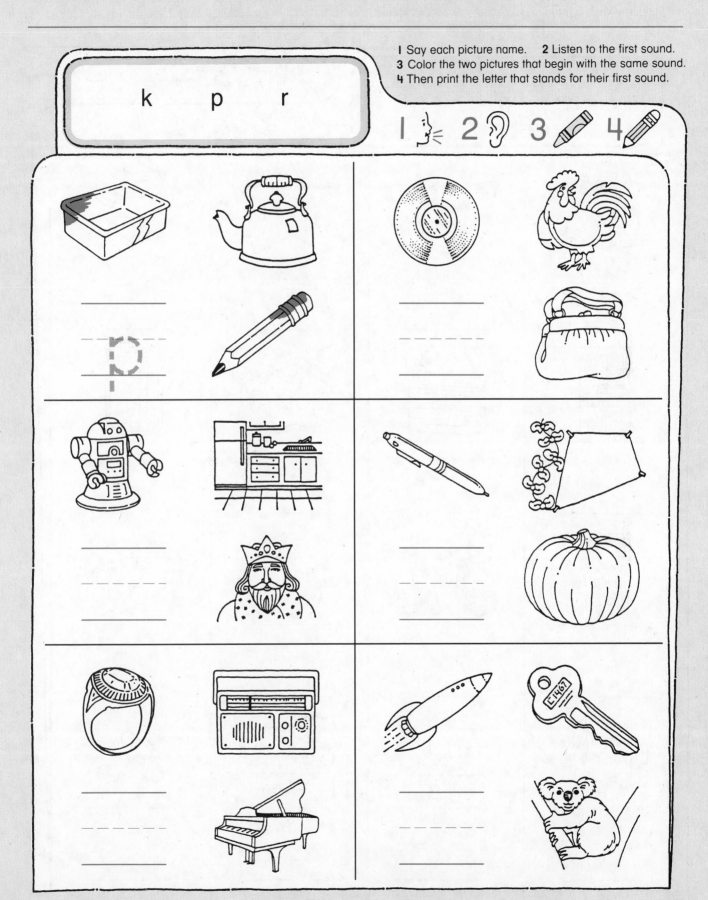

Reviewing the consonant sounds of **k**, **p**, **r** in initial position

k p r

1 Say each picture name.
2 Listen to the last sound.
3 Print the letter that stands for that sound.

1 😐 2 👂 3 ✏️

74

1 Say each picture name.
2 Listen to the first and last sounds.
3 Print the letters that stand for the first and last sounds you hear.

1 👄 2 👂 3 ✏️

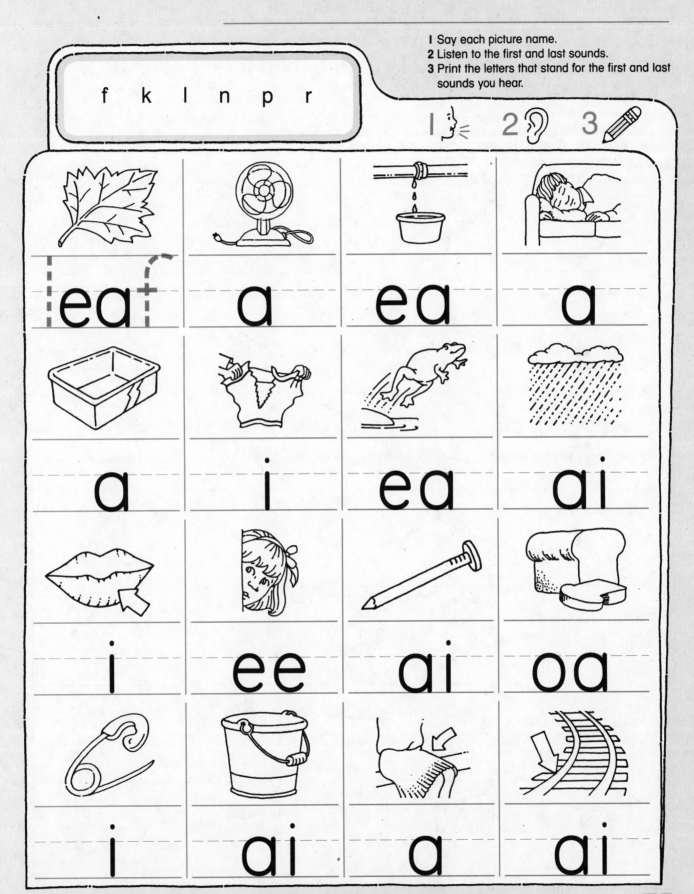

l e a f

f a

e a

n a

n a

r i

s e a

r ai

l i

j ee

n ai

l oa

p i

p ai

r a

r ai

Reviewing the consonant sounds of **f, k, l, n, p, r** in initial and final positions

a b c d e f g h i j k l m n o p q r s t u v w x y z

Directions: Say the name of the picture. Listen to the sound. Fill in the space below
each picture that has the same beginning sound as the picture in the box.

Example

Testing the consonant sounds of **f, k, l, n, p, r**; using an adapted standardized test format

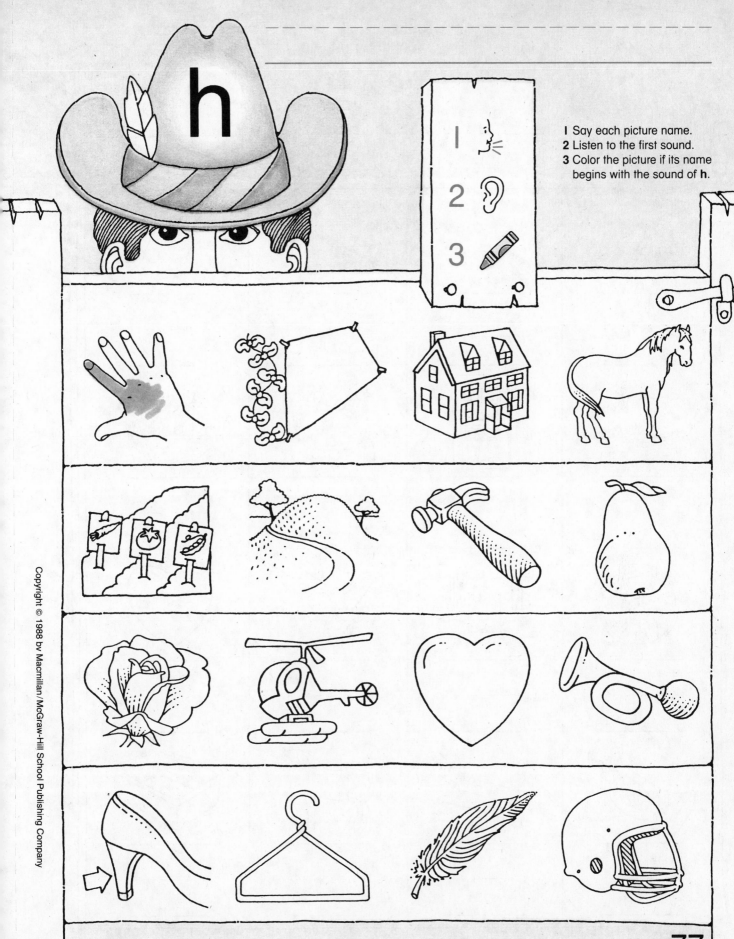

1 Say each picture name.
2 Listen to the first sound.
3 Color the picture if its name begins with the sound of **h**.

Introducing the consonant sound of **h**

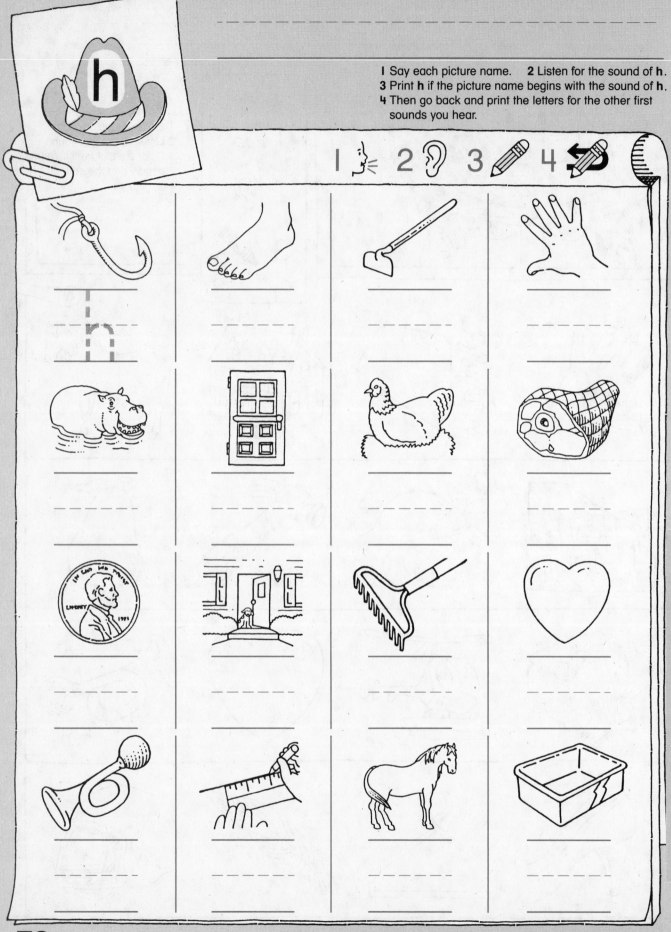

1 Say each picture name.   2 Listen for the sound of **h**.
3 Print **h** if the picture name begins with the sound of **h**.
4 Then go back and print the letters for the other first sounds you hear.

78

Using the consonant sound of **h** in initial position

j

1 Say each picture name.
2 Listen to the first sound.
3 Color the picture if its name begins with the sound of **j**.

Introducing the consonant sound of **j**

1 Say each picture name. 2 Listen for the sound of **j**.
3 Print **j** if the picture name begins with the sound of **j**.
4 Then go back and print the letters for the other first
sounds you hear.

80

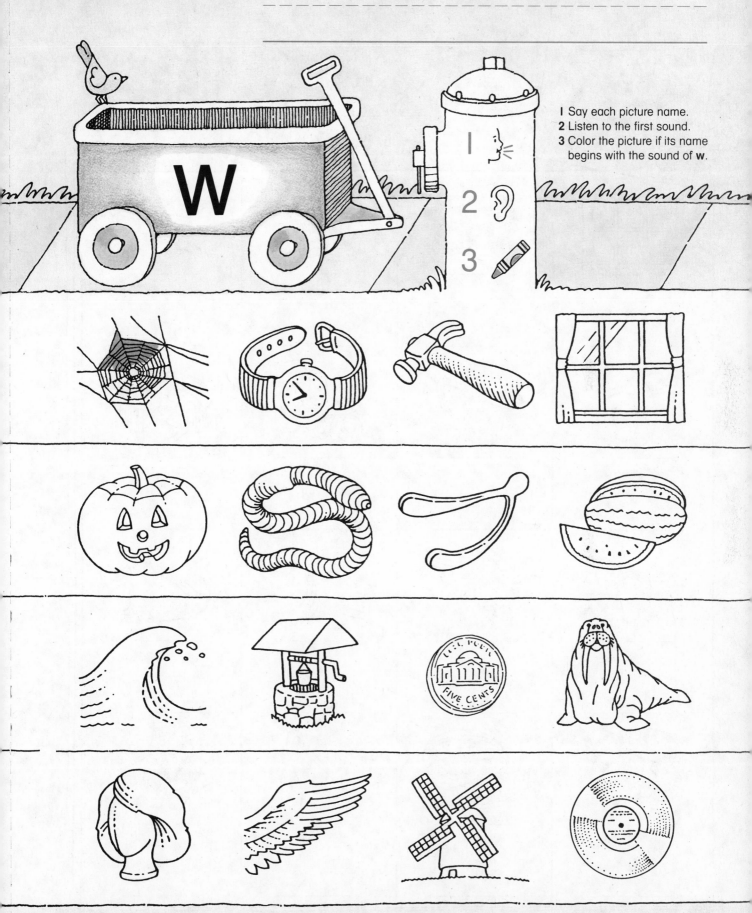

1 Say each picture name.
2 Listen to the first sound.
3 Color the picture if its name begins with the sound of **w**.

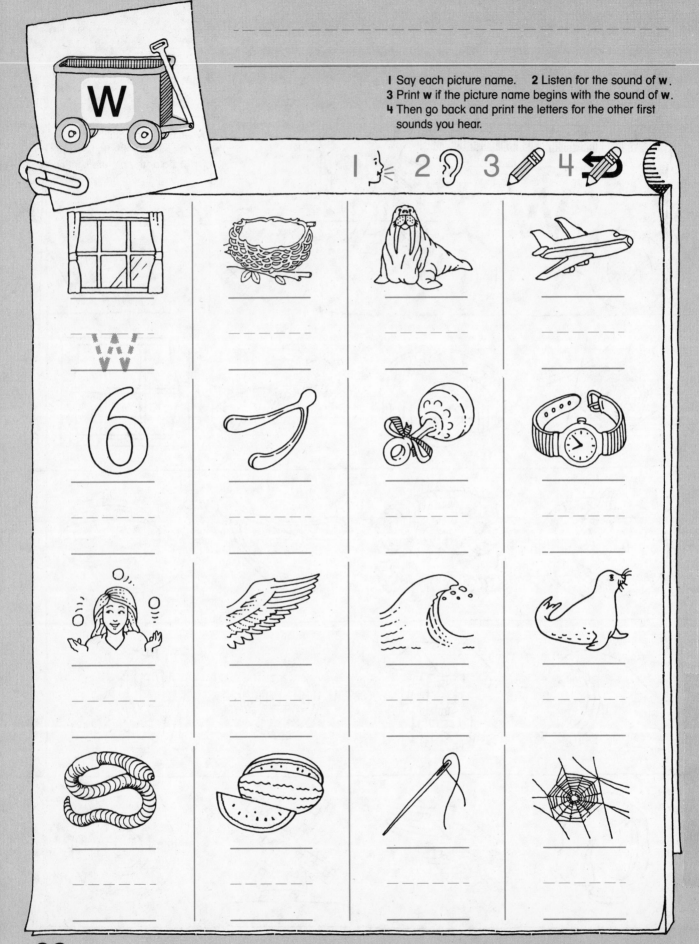

Say each picture name.   2 Listen for the sound of **w**.
3 Print **w** if the picture name begins with the sound of **w**.
4 Then go back and print the letters for the other first
   sounds you hear.

Using the consonant sound of **w** in initial position

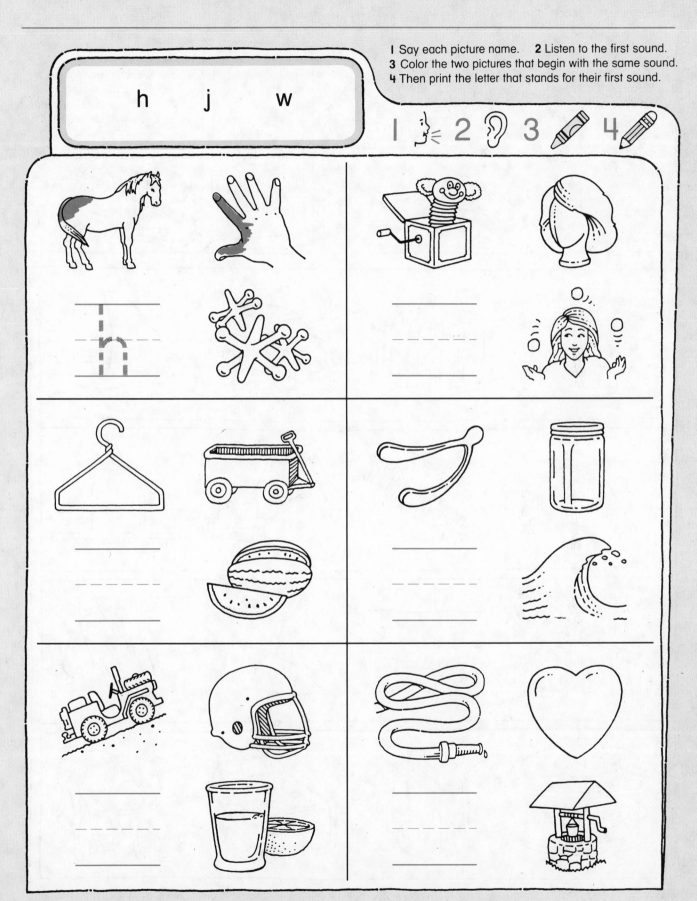

h   j   w

1 Say each picture name. 2 Listen to the first sound.
3 Color the two pictures that begin with the same sound.
4 Then print the letter that stands for their first sound.

Reviewing the consonant sounds of **h**, **j**, **w** in initial position

83

C

1 Say each picture name.
2 Listen to the first sound.
3 Color the picture if its name begins with the sound of **c**.

Introducing the consonant sound of **c**

1 Say each picture name.   2 Listen for the sound of **c**.
3 Print **c** if the picture name begins with the sound of **c**.
4 Then go back and print the letters for the other first
   sounds you hear.

1 2 3 4

Using the consonant sound of **c** in initial position

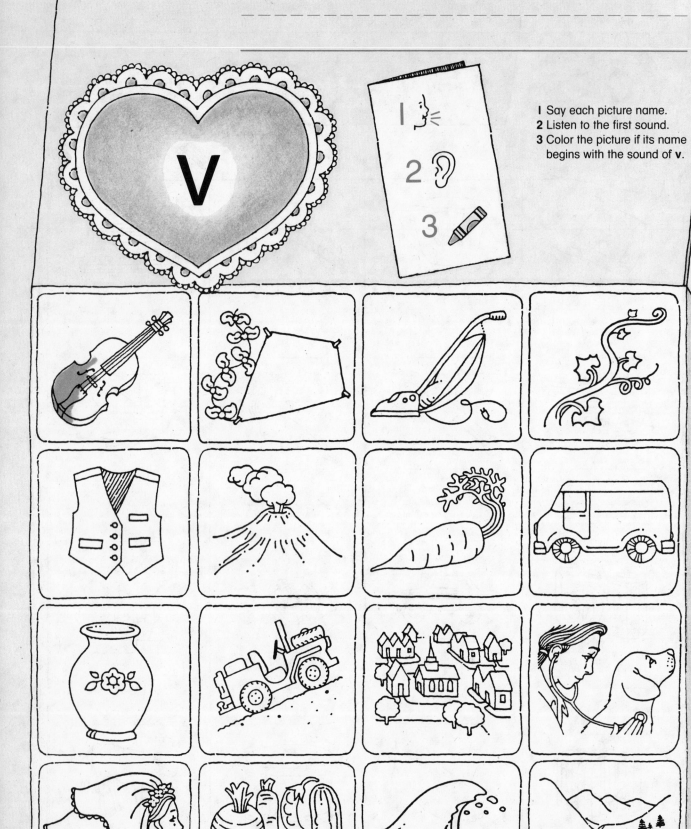

1 Say each picture name.
2 Listen to the first sound.
3 Color the picture if its name begins with the sound of **v**.

V

1 Say each picture name. 2 Listen for the sound of **v**.
3 Print **v** if the picture name begins with the sound of **v**.
4 Then go back and print the letters for the other first sounds you hear.

1 🗣️ 2 👂 3 ✏️ 4 ↩️✏️

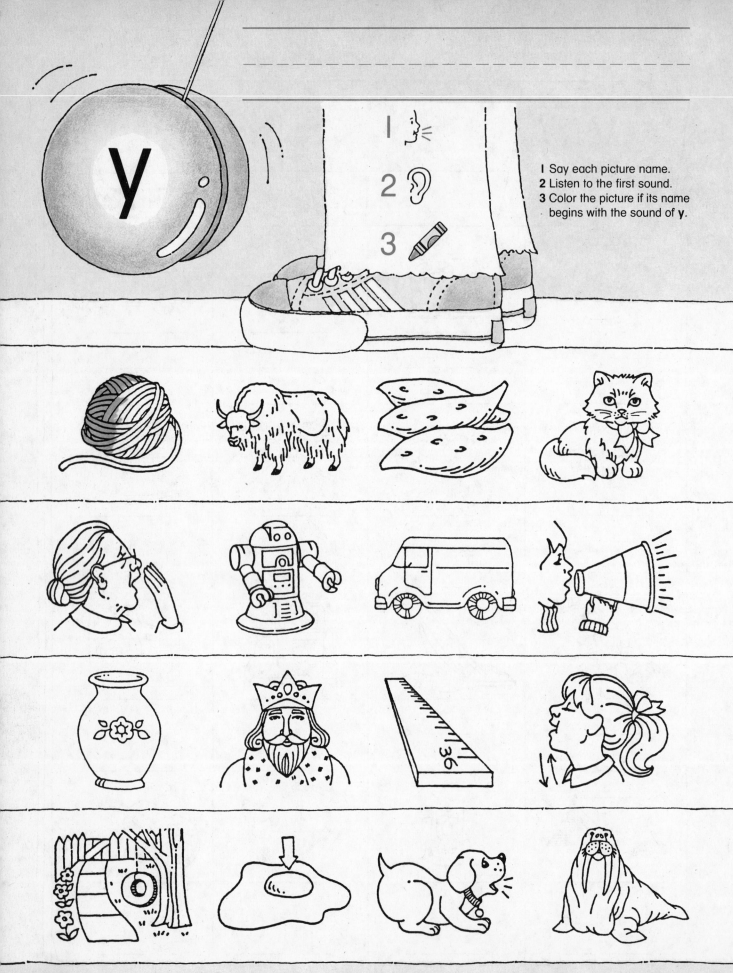

1 Say each picture name.
2 Listen to the first sound.
3 Color the picture if its name begins with the sound of **y**.

Introducing the consonant sound of **y**

1 Say each picture name.   2 Listen to the first sound.
3 Color the two pictures that begin with the same sound.
4 Then print the letter that stands for their first sound.

c   v   y

1   2   3   4

Reviewing the consonant sounds of **c**, **v**, **y** in initial position

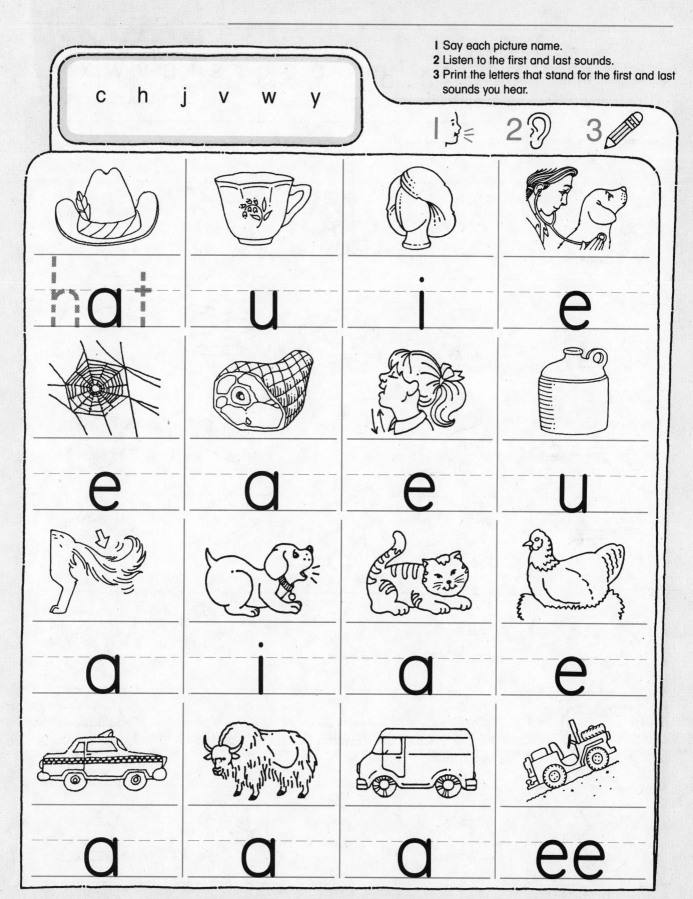

c h j v w y

1 Say each picture name.
2 Listen to the first and last sounds.
3 Print the letters that stand for the first and last sounds you hear.

1 2 3

h a t
u
i
e

e
a
e
u

a
i
a
e

a
a
a
ee

Reviewing the consonant sounds of **c, h, j, v, w, y** in initial and final position a b **c** d e f g **h** i **j** k l m n o p q r s t u **v** **w** x y z

Directions: Say the name of the picture. Listen to the sound. Fill in the space below each picture that has the same beginning sound as the picture in the box.

Example

Testing the consonant sounds of **c**, **h**, **j**, **v**, **w**, **y**; using an adapted standardized test format

1 Say each picture name.
2 Listen to the first sound.
3 Color the picture if its name begins with the sound of **qu**.

1 Say each picture name. **2** Listen for the sound of **qu**.
3 Print **qu** if the picture name begins with the sound of **qu**.
4 Then go back and print the letters for the other first
     sounds you hear.

1 2 3 4

94

1 Say each picture name.
2 Listen to the first sound.
3 Color the picture if its name begins with the sound of **z**.

0,1,2

10364

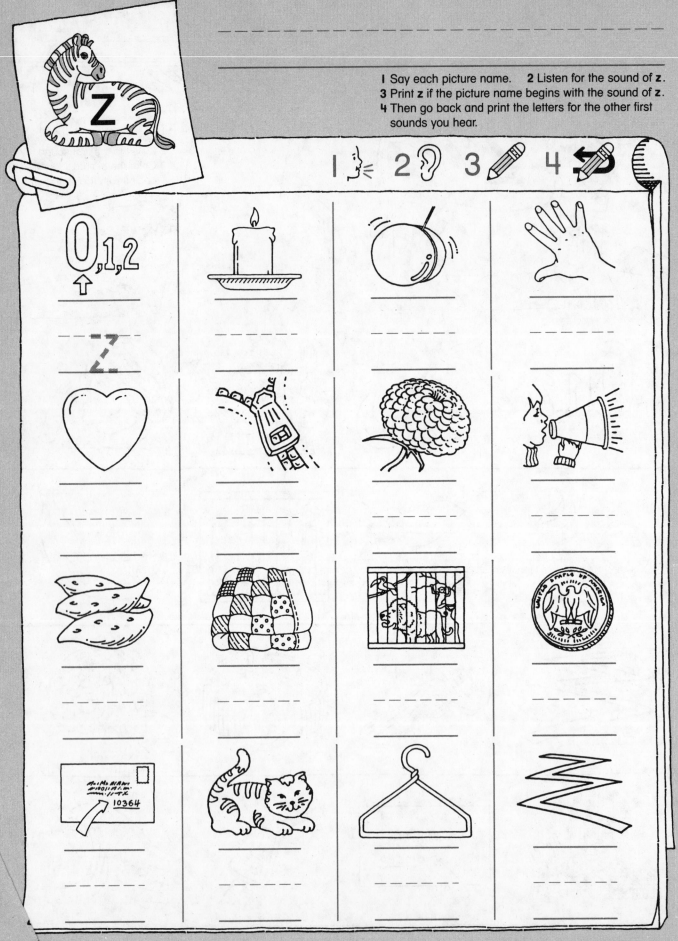

1 Say each picture name. 2 Listen for the sound of **z**.
3 Print **z** if the picture name begins with the sound of **z**.
4 Then go back and print the letters for the other first sounds you hear.

1 𝕝ﹳ 2 👂 3 ✏ 4 ↩✏

96

Using the consonant sound of **z** in initial position

1 Say each picture name.
2 Listen to the last sound.
3 Color the picture if its name ends with the sound of **x**.

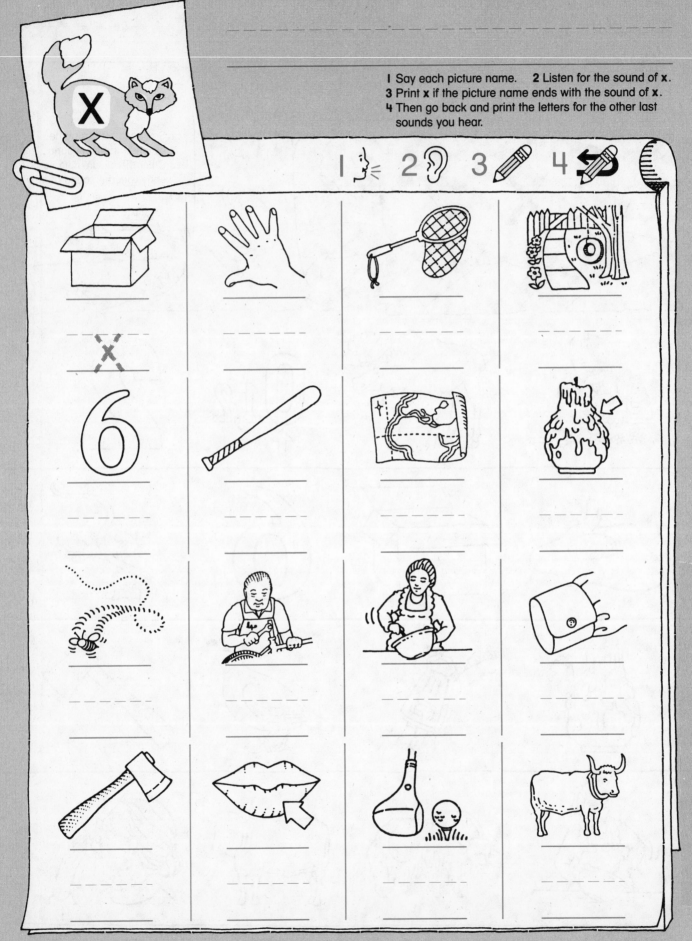

1 Say each picture name.   2 Listen for the sound of **x**.
3 Print **x** if the picture name ends with the sound of **x**.
4 Then go back and print the letters for the other last
   sounds you hear.

1   2   3   4

98

1 Say each picture name.
2 Listen to the first sound and last sound. 3 Color the two pictures that begin or end with the same sound.
4 Then print the letter or letters that stand for that sound.

1 | 2 | 3 | 4

qu

0,1,2

6

Reviewing the consonant sounds of **qu**, **x**, **z**

99

1 Say each picture name.
2 Listen to the first and last sounds.
3 Print the letters that stand for the first and last sounds you hear.

1 🗣 2 👂 3 ✏️

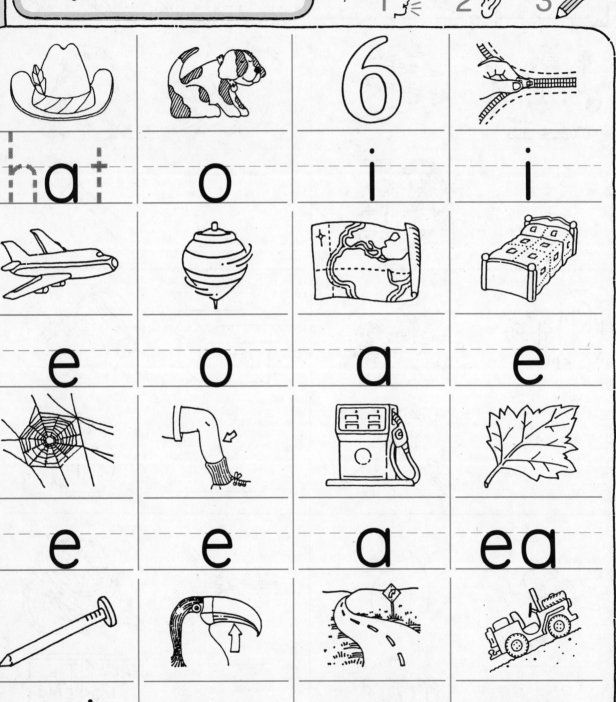

h a t

o

i

i

e

o

a

e

e

e

a

ea

ai

ea

oa

ee

100

Reviewing consonant sounds in initial and final positions

a b c d e f g h i j k l m n o p q r s t u v w x y z

Directions: Say the name of the picture. Listen to the sound. Fill in the space below
each picture that has the same beginning sound as the picture in the box.

Example

Testing the consonant sounds; using an adapted standardized test format

1 Say each picture name.
2 Listen for the short sound of **a**.
3 Color the picture if its name has the short sound of **a**.

Introducing the short sound of **a**

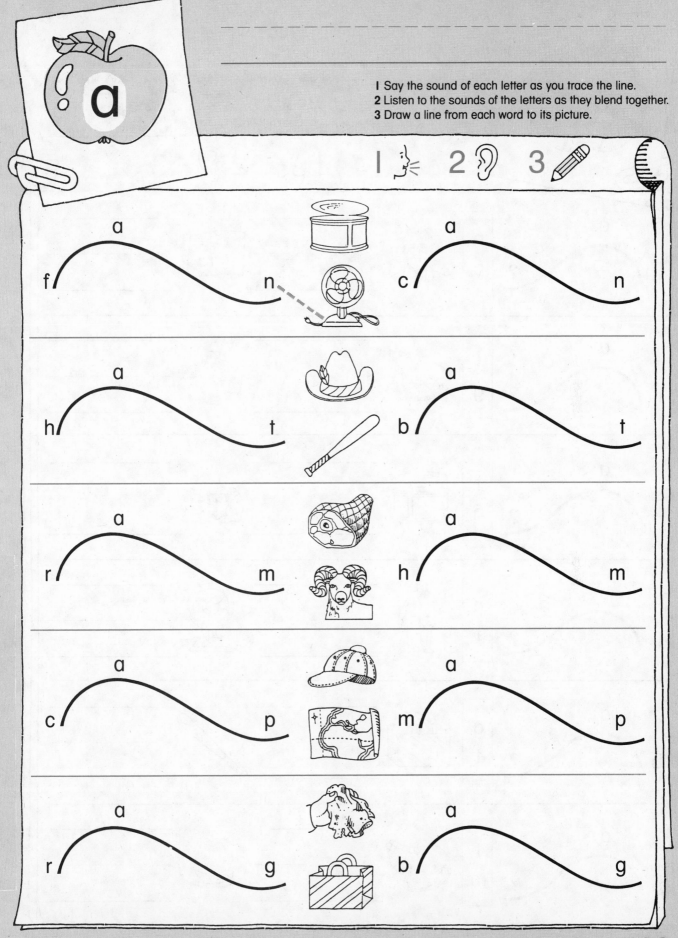

1 Say the sound of each letter as you trace the line.
2 Listen to the sounds of the letters as they blend together.
3 Draw a line from each word to its picture.

Using the short sound of **a**; blending words

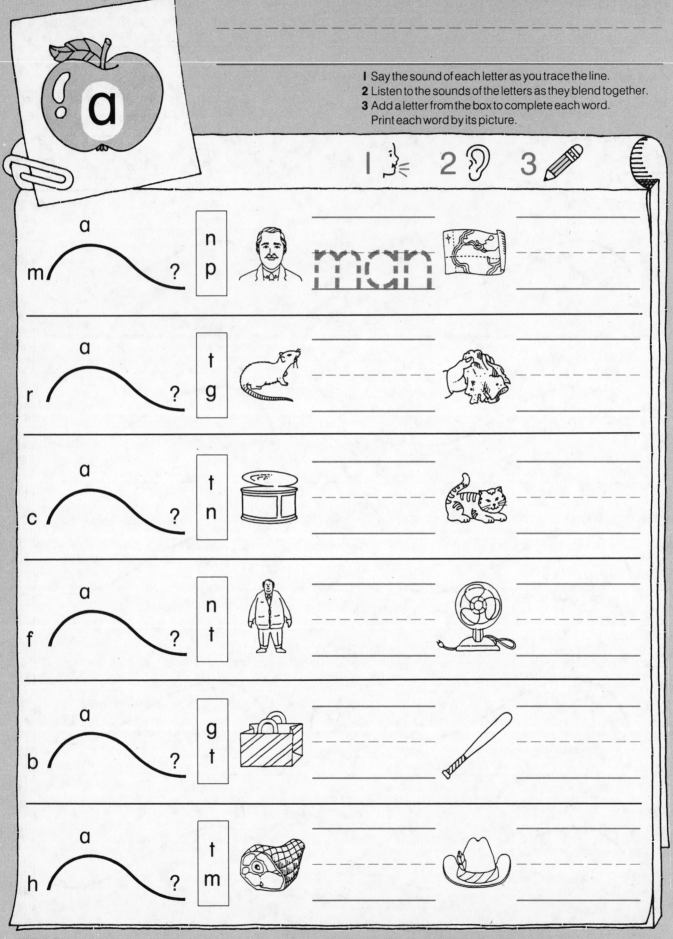

1 Say the sound of each letter as you trace the line.
2 Listen to the sounds of the letters as they blend together.
3 Add a letter from the box to complete each word.
  Print each word by its picture.

1 | 2 | 3

a
m ?   n p   man

a
r ?   t g

a
c ?   t n

a
f ?   n t

a
b ?   g t

a
h ?   t m

Using the short sound of **a**; blending words

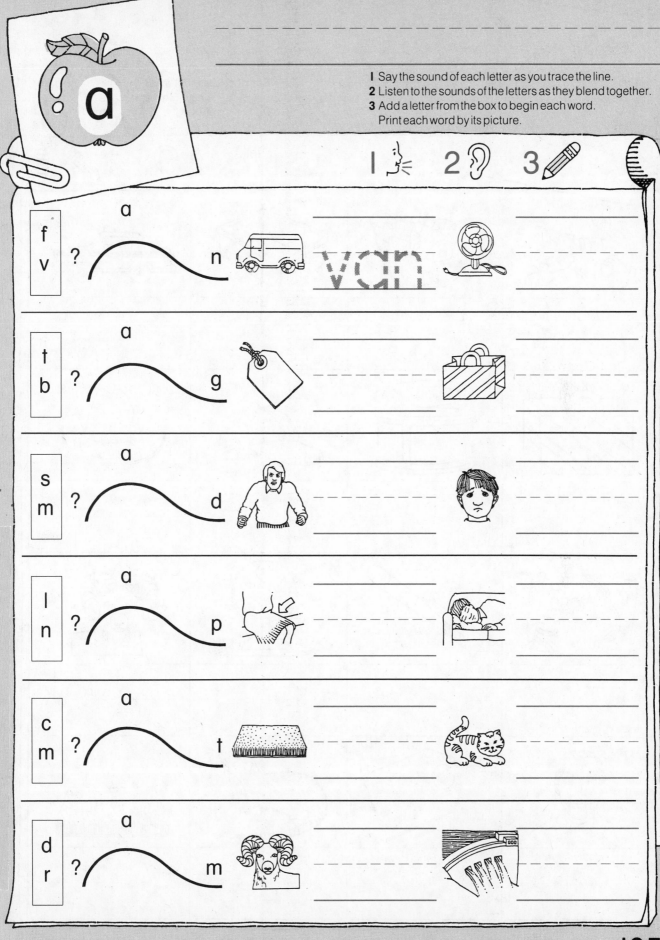

1 Say the sound of each letter as you trace the line.
2 Listen to the sounds of the letters as they blend together.
3 Add a letter from the box to begin each word.
  Print each word by its picture.

1 🗣 2 👂 3 ✏

f v ?   a   n   van

t b ?   a   g

s m ?   a   d

l n ?   a   p

c m ?   a   t

d r ?   a   m

Using the short sound of **a**; blending words

105

1 Say each picture name.
2 Listen to the sound of each letter.
3 Print the word for the picture name.

1 🗣 2 👂 3 ✏️

cat

Using the short sound of **a**; spelling words

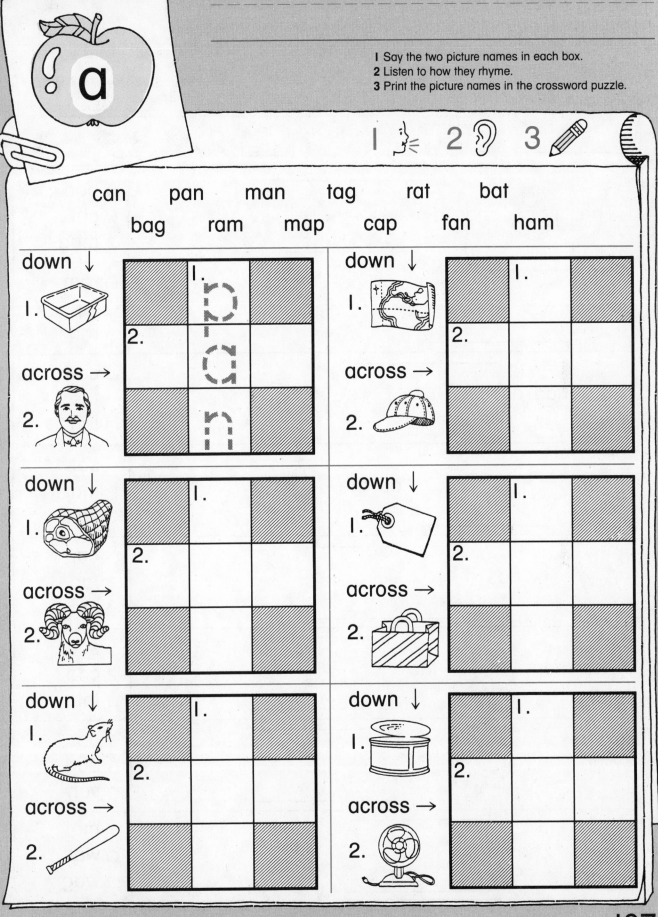

1 Say the two picture names in each box.
2 Listen to how they rhyme.
3 Print the picture names in the crossword puzzle.

1 🗣 2 👂 3 ✏️

can   pan   man   tag   rat   bat
bag   ram   map   cap   fan   ham

Using the short sound of **a**; writing rhyming words

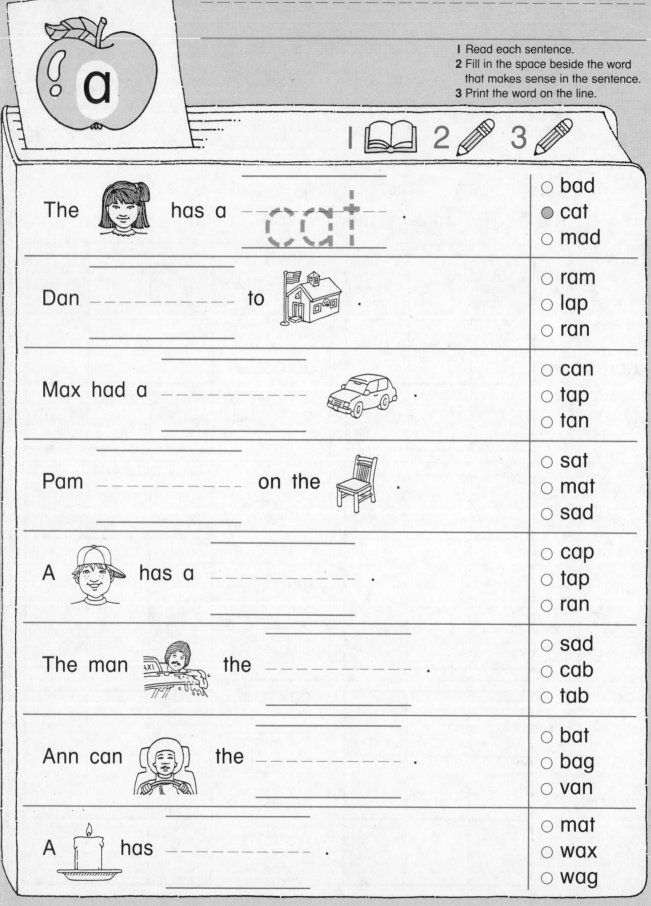

1 Read each sentence.
2 Fill in the space beside the word that makes sense in the sentence.
3 Print the word on the line.

1 📖 2 ✏️ 3 ✏️

The 👧 has a ___cat___ .
- ○ bad
- ● cat
- ○ mad

Dan _____ to 🏫 .
- ○ ram
- ○ lap
- ○ ran

Max had a _____ 🚗 .
- ○ can
- ○ tap
- ○ tan

Pam _____ on the 🪑 .
- ○ sat
- ○ mat
- ○ sad

A 🧢👦 has a _____ .
- ○ cap
- ○ tap
- ○ ran

The man _____ the _____ .
- ○ sad
- ○ cab
- ○ tab

Ann can _____ the _____ .
- ○ bat
- ○ bag
- ○ van

A 🕯️ has _____ .
- ○ mat
- ○ wax
- ○ wag

Language arts applications: using sentence context to select words with the short sound of **a**

 1 2

Dad has a hat.
Dad has a ham.

Dad has a hat.

The cat sat on a mat.
The cat sat on a lap.

Jan has a pan.
Jan has a bat.

Dad sat in the cab.
Pam sat in the van.

The can has a tag.
The fan has a tag.

1 Read the story below. 2 Say each word.
3 Listen carefully for the short sound of **a**.
4 Draw a line under each word with the short sound of **a**.

1 📖   2 🗣   3 👂   4 ✏️

Pam has a cat.
That cat is Sam.

Pam has a hat.
Sam sat on the hat.

Pam has a fan.
Sam had a nap on the fan.

Pam got mad at Sam.
"Bad Sam. Keep off my hat and fan.
You can nap on my lap."

Language arts applications: reading a story with words with the short sound of **a**

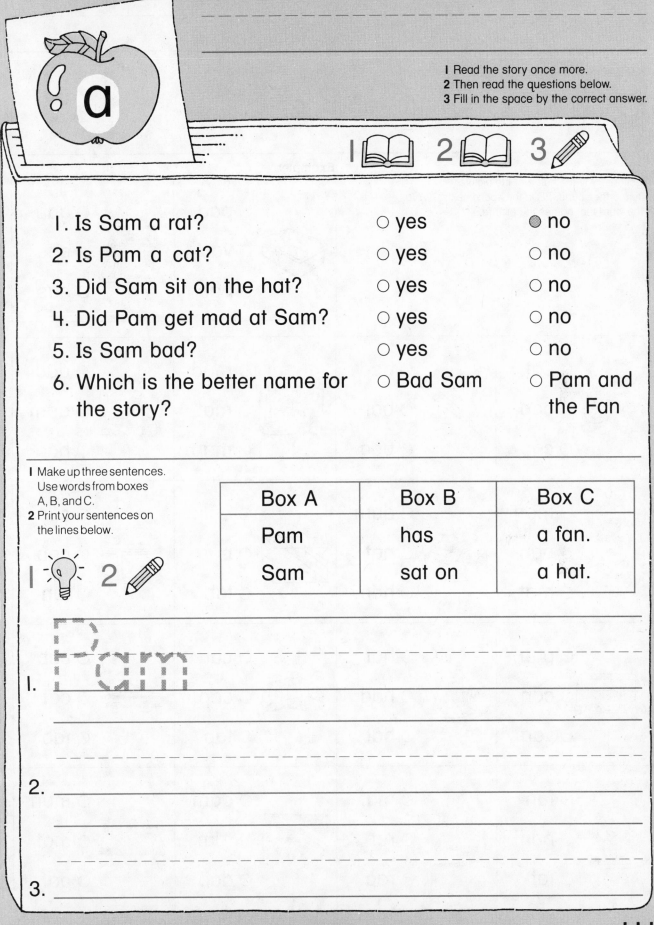

1 Read the story once more.
2 Then read the questions below.
3 Fill in the space by the correct answer.

1 📖 2 📖 3 ✏️

1. Is Sam a rat? ○ yes ● no
2. Is Pam a cat? ○ yes ○ no
3. Did Sam sit on the hat? ○ yes ○ no
4. Did Pam get mad at Sam? ○ yes ○ no
5. Is Sam bad? ○ yes ○ no
6. Which is the better name for the story? ○ Bad Sam ○ Pam and the Fan

1 Make up three sentences. Use words from boxes A, B, and C.
2 Print your sentences on the lines below.

1 💡 2 ✏️

Box A	Box B	Box C
Pam	has	a fan.
Sam	sat on	a hat.

1. Pam _____

2. _____

3. _____

a e i o u

Directions: Say the name of the picture. Listen to the sound. Fill in the space next to the word that names the picture.

Examples

	○ pad ○ van ○ pan		○ gab ○ gas ○ has

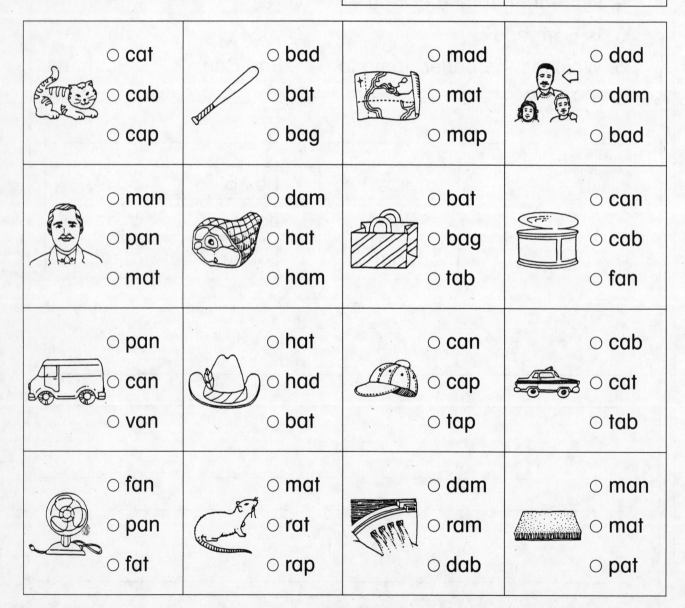

○ cat ○ cab ○ cap	○ bad ○ bat ○ bag	○ mad ○ mat ○ map	○ dad ○ dam ○ bad
○ man ○ pan ○ mat	○ dam ○ hat ○ ham	○ bat ○ bag ○ tab	○ can ○ cab ○ fan
○ pan ○ can ○ van	○ hat ○ had ○ bat	○ can ○ cap ○ tap	○ cab ○ cat ○ tab
○ fan ○ pan ○ fat	○ mat ○ rat ○ rap	○ dam ○ ram ○ dab	○ man ○ mat ○ pat

Testing the short sound of **a**; using an adapted standardized test format

1 Say each picture name.
2 Listen for the short sound of **i**.
3 Color the picture if its name has the short sound of **i**.

Introducing the short sound of **i**

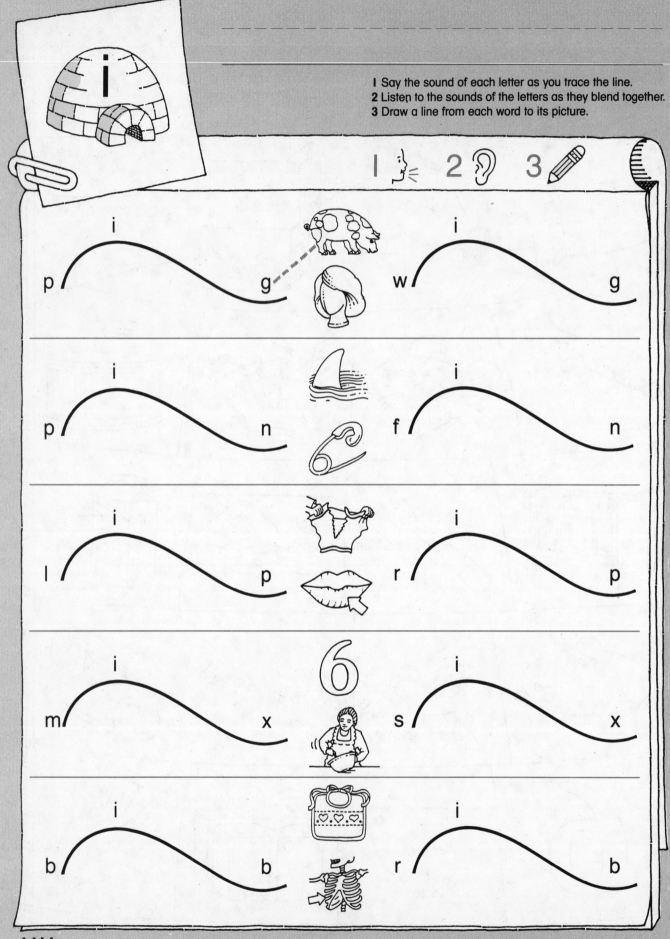

1 Say the sound of each letter as you trace the line.
2 Listen to the sounds of the letters as they blend together.
3 Draw a line from each word to its picture.

1   2   3

114

Using the short sound of **i**; blending words

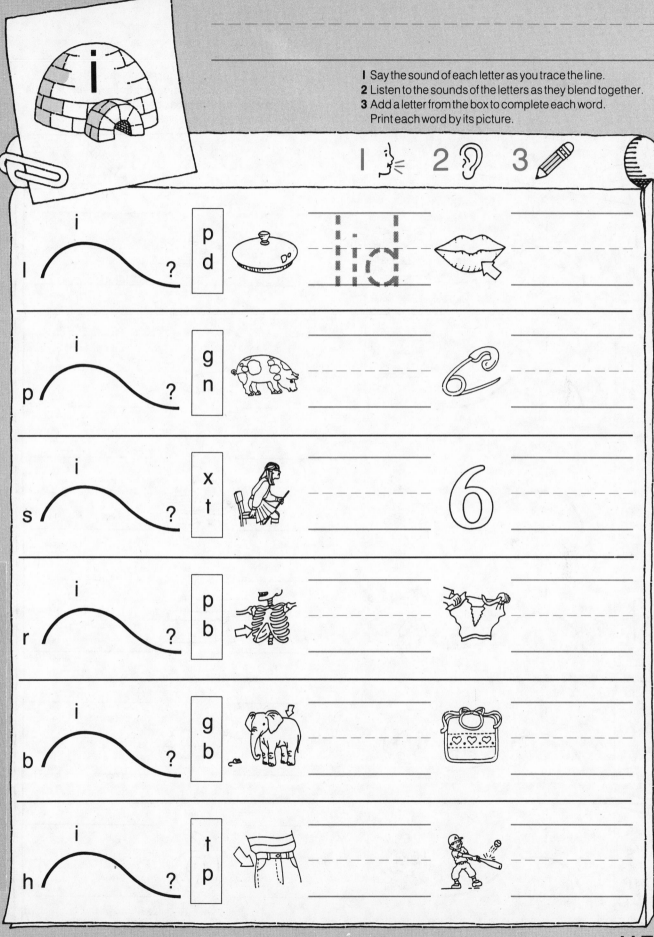

1 Say the sound of each letter as you trace the line.
2 Listen to the sounds of the letters as they blend together.
3 Add a letter from the box to complete each word.
   Print each word by its picture.

lid

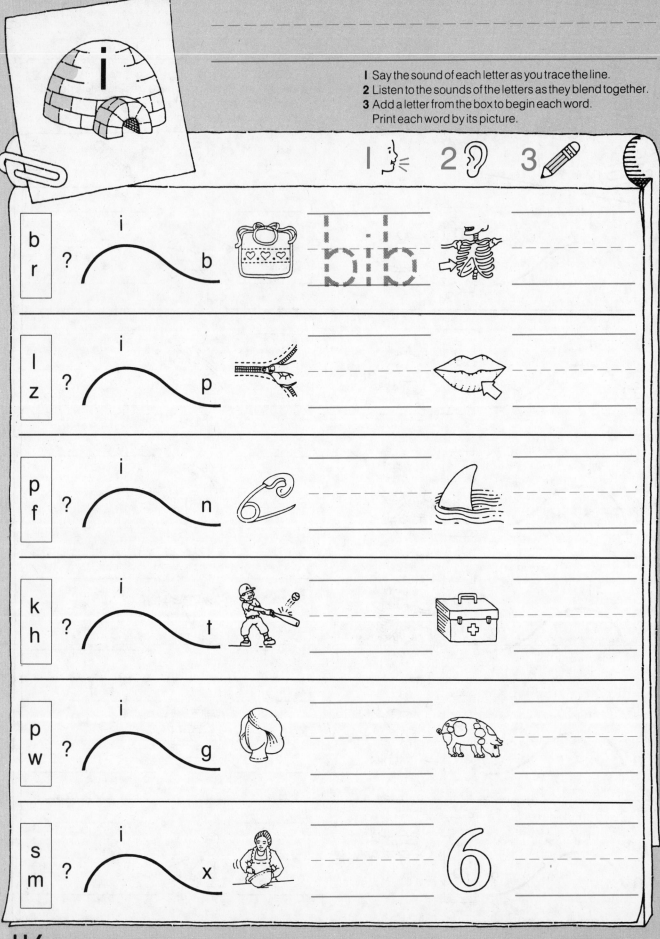

1 Say the sound of each letter as you trace the line.
2 Listen to the sounds of the letters as they blend together.
3 Add a letter from the box to begin each word.
   Print each word by its picture.

b
r ? i b   bib

l
z ? i p

p
f ? i n

k
h ? i t

p
w ? i g

s
m ? i x   6

116

Using the short sound of **i**; blending words

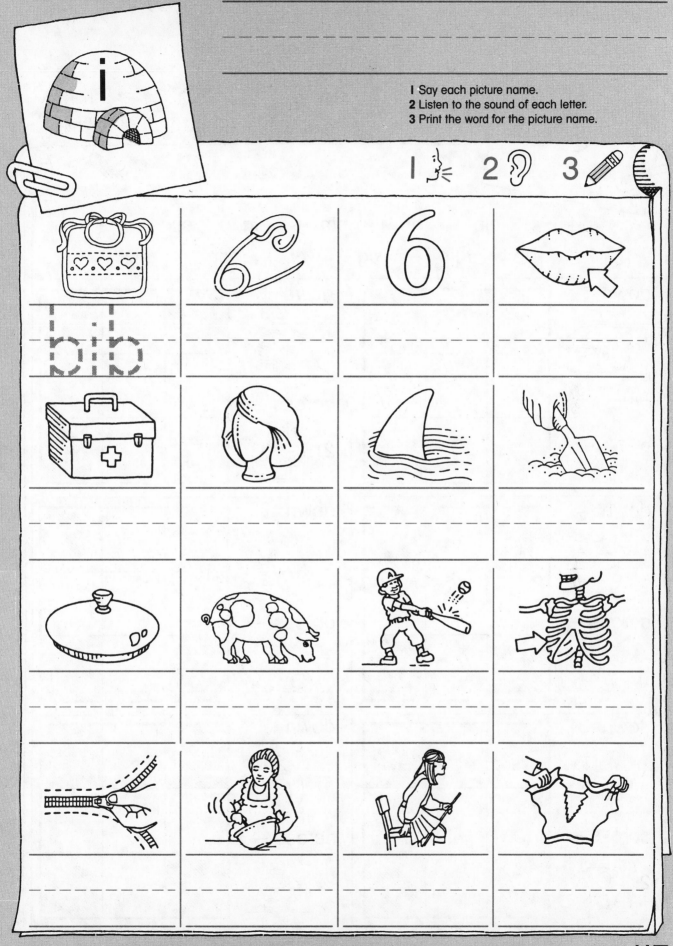

1 Say each picture name.
2 Listen to the sound of each letter.
3 Print the word for the picture name.

1 2 3

bib

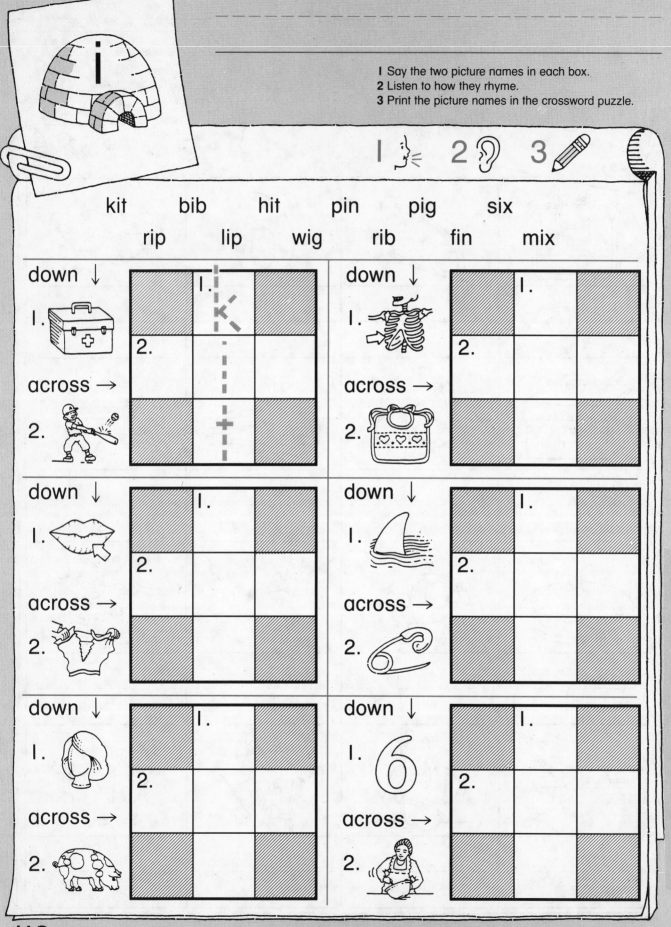

1 Say the two picture names in each box.
2 Listen to how they rhyme.
3 Print the picture names in the crossword puzzle.

kit   bib   hit   pin   pig   six
rip   lip   wig   rib   fin   mix

down ↓

1.

2.

across →

2.

down ↓

1.

2.

across →

2.

down ↓

1.

2.

across →

2.

down ↓

1.

2.

across →

2.

down ↓

1.

2.

across →

2.

down ↓

1.

2.

across →

2.

Using the short sound of **i**; writing rhyming words

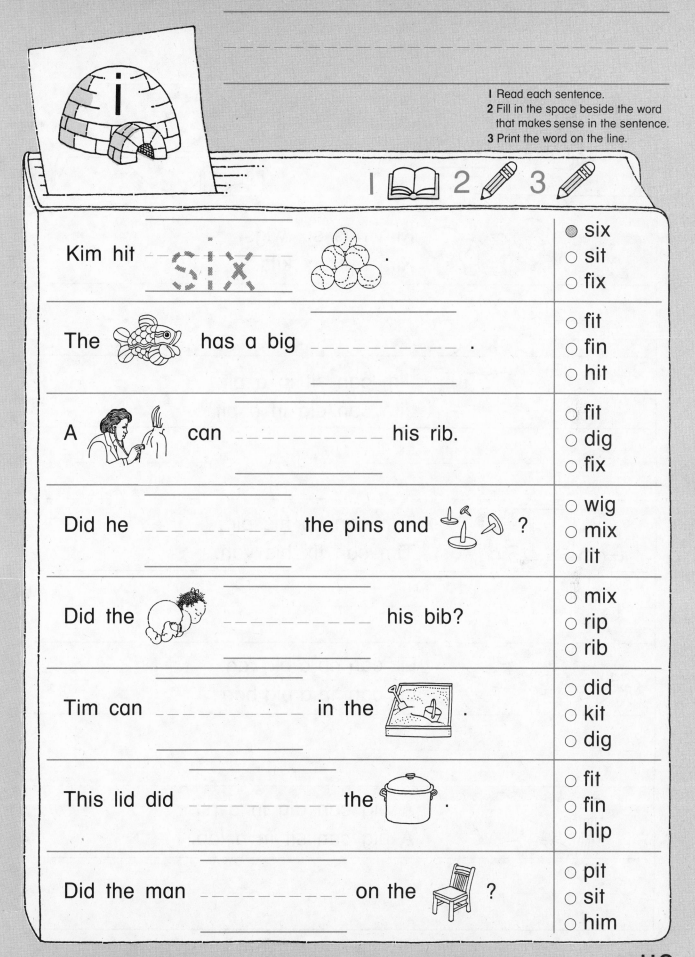

Read each sentence.
Fill in the space beside the word that makes sense in the sentence.
Print the word on the line.

1. Read each sentence.
2. Fill in the space beside the word that makes sense in the sentence.
3. Print the word on the line.

Kim hit six .
- ● six
- ○ sit
- ○ fix

The 🐟 has a big _____ .
- ○ fit
- ○ fin
- ○ hit

A can _____ his rib.
- ○ fit
- ○ dig
- ○ fix

Did he _____ the pins and ?
- ○ wig
- ○ mix
- ○ lit

Did the _____ his bib?
- ○ mix
- ○ rip
- ○ rib

Tim can _____ in the .
- ○ did
- ○ kit
- ○ dig

This lid did _____ the .
- ○ fit
- ○ fin
- ○ hip

Did the man _____ on the ?
- ○ pit
- ○ sit
- ○ him

Language arts applications: using sentence context to select words with the short sound of i

Language arts applications: using sentence context to select words with the short sound of i

119

Kim has six wigs.
Kim hid six kits.

Kim has six wigs.

Jim can sit in a pit.
Jim can dig in a pit.

Tim can tip his pig.
Tim can fix his van.

Liz can rip a big rag.
Liz can tip a big bag.

A pig can dig in a pit.
A pig can sit in a lap.

120

Language arts applications: using the short sound of **i** to select sentences from context

 I Read the story below. **2** Say each word.
3 Listen carefully for the short sound of **i**.
4 Draw a line under each word with the short sound of **i**.

Vic had a big pig. Vic called the pig Sis.

One day Sis saw a wig. She put on this wig.

Lil saw the pig. She said, "You are a funny pig, Sis.
This is my wig. It does not fit you.
It is not for a pig."

Sis was sad. She hid in her pen.

Lil said, "Come here, Sis. You can have this wig.
I can fix it for you. I can make it fit."

Lil put a pin in the wig. Then the wig fit Sis.

1 Read the story once more.
2 Then read the questions below.
3 Fill in the space by the correct answer.

 1 2 3

1. Did Vic have a pig? ● yes   ○ no
2. Did Vic have a wig? ○ yes   ○ no
3. Did the wig fit the pig? ○ yes   ○ no
4. Did Lil fix the wig? ○ yes   ○ no
5. Should a pig have a wig? ○ yes   ○ no
6. Which is the better name for the story?   ○ A Wig for Sis   ○ Sis Has a Pig

1 Make up three sentences. Use words from boxes A, B, and C.
2 Print your sentences on the lines below.

 1   2

Box A	Box B	Box C
Lil	has	a wig.
Vic	can fix	a pig.

1. _____

_____

2. _____

_____

3. _____

Language arts applications: story comprehension; writing sentences using words with the short sound of **i**

a e [i] o u

Directions: Say the name of the picture. Listen to the sound. Fill in the space next to the word that names the picture.

Examples

○ fin	○ dig
○ pin	○ dip
○ pit	○ pig

○ lip ○ hid ○ lid	○ zip ○ hip ○ his	○ six ○ sit ○ hit	○ tip ○ sip ○ six
○ fix ○ fin ○ mix	○ wig ○ win ○ pig	○ bib ○ rib ○ rid	○ lit ○ tip ○ lip
○ bit ○ bib ○ bid	○ six ○ mix ○ sit	○ rim ○ zip ○ rip	○ pig ○ pit ○ big
○ kid ○ kit ○ hit	○ pin ○ fit ○ fin	○ him ○ sit ○ hit	○ pit ○ pig ○ fit

Testing the short sound of **i**; using an adapted standardized test format

O

1 Say each picture name.
2 Listen for the short sound of **o**.
3 Color the picture if its name has the short sound of **o**.

124

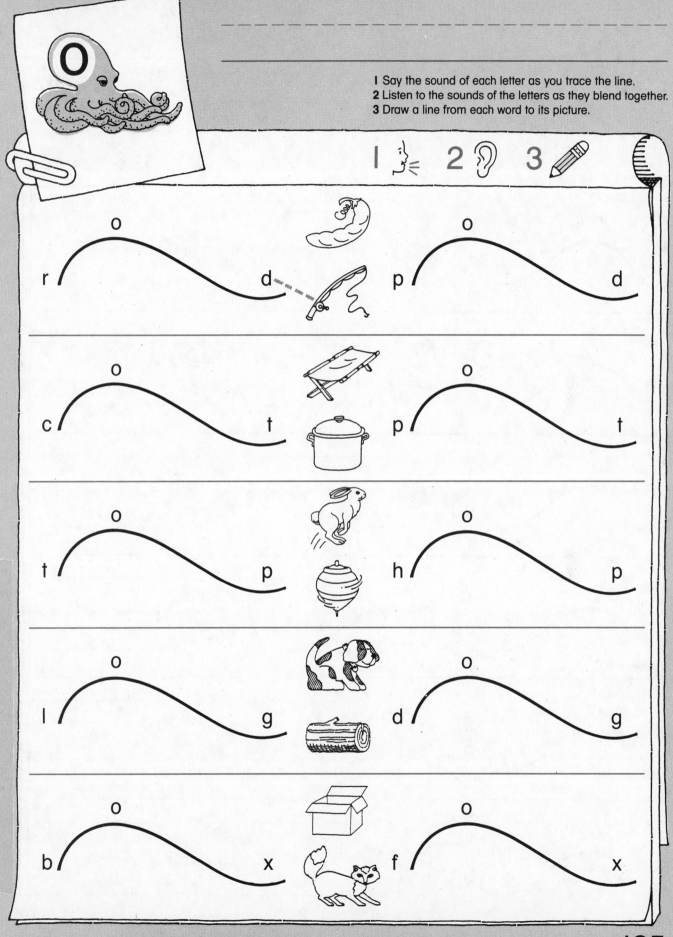

1 Say the sound of each letter as you trace the line.
2 Listen to the sounds of the letters as they blend together.
3 Draw a line from each word to its picture.

Using the short sound of **o**; blending words

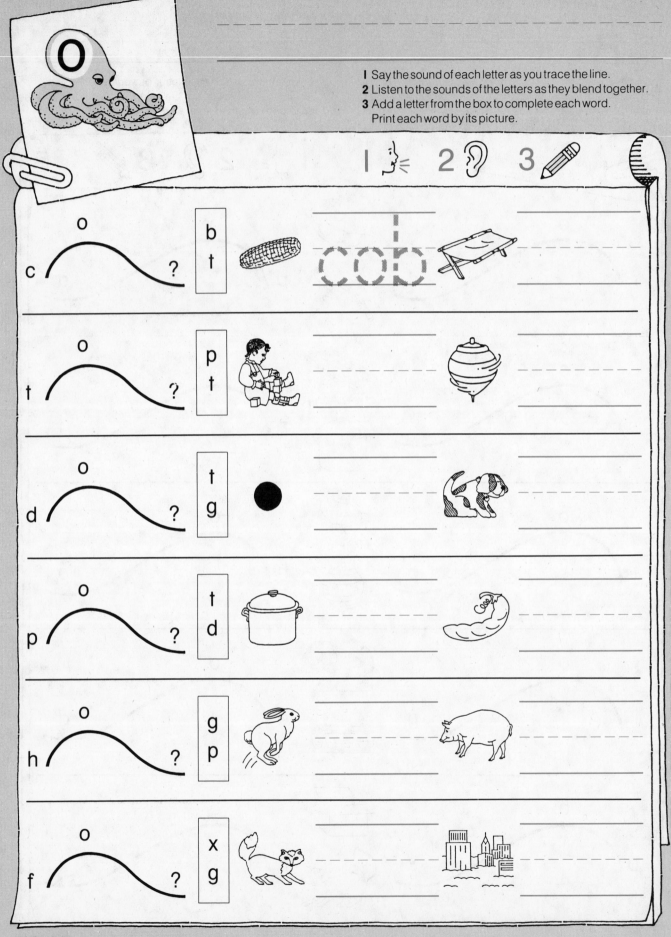

o

1 Say the sound of each letter as you trace the line.
2 Listen to the sounds of the letters as they blend together.
3 Add a letter from the box to complete each word.
Print each word by its picture.

1 | 2 | 3

o

c ? | b
       t

cob

o

t ? | p
       t

o

d ? | t
       g

o

p ? | t
       d

o

h ? | g
       p

o

f ? | x
       g

126

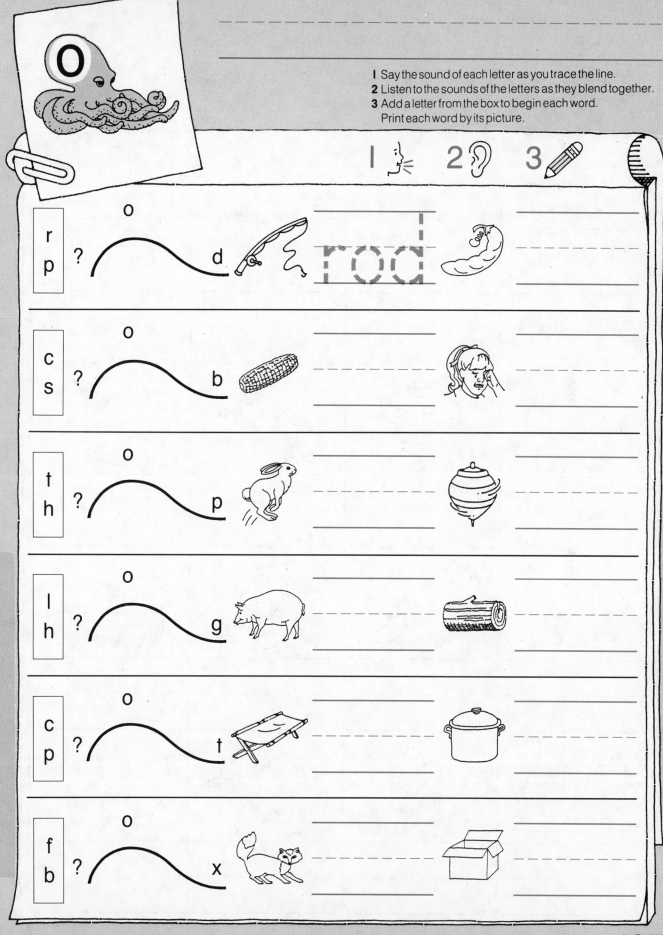

1 Say the sound of each letter as you trace the line.
2 Listen to the sounds of the letters as they blend together.
3 Add a letter from the box to begin each word.
Print each word by its picture.

rod

1 Say each picture name.
2 Listen to the sound of each letter.
3 Print the word for the picture name.

pot

Using the short sound of **o**; spelling words

1 Say the two picture names in each box.
2 Listen to how they rhyme.
3 Print the picture names in the crossword puzzle.

1 🗣 2 👂 3 ✏️

pot   cob   rod   top   log   fox
  hog   cot   pop   box   pod   sob

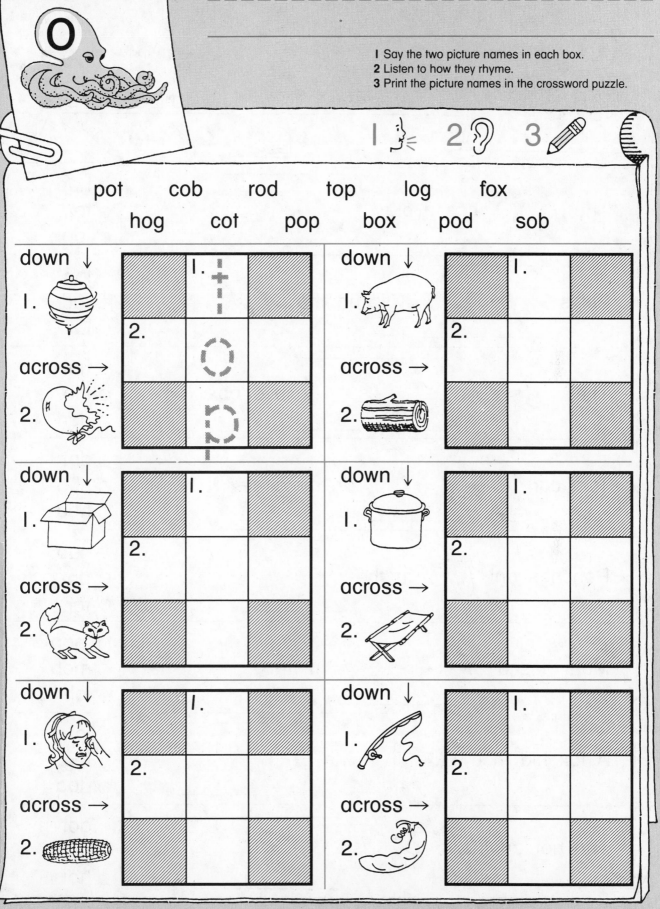

down ↓

1.

across →

2.

down ↓

1.

across →

2.

down ↓

1.

across →

2.

down ↓

1.

across →

2.

down ↓

1.

across →

2.

down ↓

1.

across →

2.

1 Read each sentence.
2 Fill in the space beside the word that makes sense in the sentence.
3 Print the word on the line.

The [image] has a big **top** .

- ○ hop
- ○ tot
- ● top

Bob's _____ is on the [image] .

- ○ log
- ○ rod
- ○ lot

The [image] is _____ in a box.

- ○ not
- ○ job
- ○ nod

Tom can _____ on his [image] .

- ○ dot
- ○ hop
- ○ hog

Ron has an [image] in the _____ .

- ○ sob
- ○ pot
- ○ top

Mom has a _____ in her [image] .

- ○ mop
- ○ mob
- ○ job

A fox hid in a [image] in the _____ .

- ○ lot
- ○ log
- ○ dog

The pot on the [image] is _____ .

- ○ got
- ○ hog
- ○ hot

130

 1 2

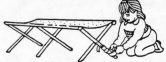

Dot can fix the pot.
Dot can fix the cot.

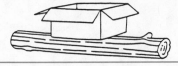

The fox is on the log.
The box is on the log.

_____

Bob hid a mop in a box.
Bob hid a top in a box.

_____

The hog bit a big dog.
The hog bit a big cob.

_____

A dog ran at the fox.
A dog will hop in the box.

_____

Language arts applications: using the short sound of **o** to select sentences from context

O

1 Read the story below.　**2** Say each word.
3 Listen carefully for the short sound of **o**.
4 Draw a line under each word with the short sound of **o**.

A fox put a pot on a log. A hog came by.
"What is in the pot?" asked the hog.
"Is it a cob?"

"No," said the fox.

"Is it a ham?"

"No," said the fox.

"Is it an ox?"

"No."

Then the fox got the lid off the pot.
"There is fog in this pot," said the fox.
"Pop your head in and see."

"No," said the hog.
"I will not pop my head in the pot.
You may eat fog.
You will not eat this hog."

132

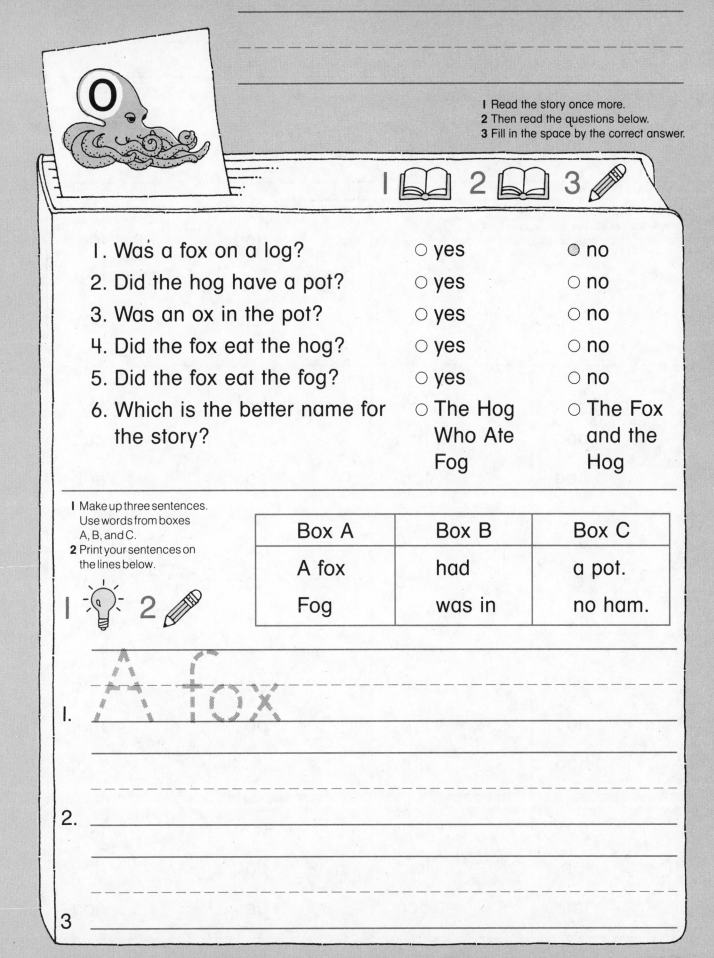

1 Read the story once more.
2 Then read the questions below.
3 Fill in the space by the correct answer.

1 📖 2 📖 3 ✏️

1. Was a fox on a log? ○ yes ● no
2. Did the hog have a pot? ○ yes ○ no
3. Was an ox in the pot? ○ yes ○ no
4. Did the fox eat the hog? ○ yes ○ no
5. Did the fox eat the fog? ○ yes ○ no
6. Which is the better name for the story? ○ The Hog Who Ate Fog ○ The Fox and the Hog

1 Make up three sentences. Use words from boxes A, B, and C.
2 Print your sentences on the lines below.

1 💡 2 ✏️

Box A	Box B	Box C
A fox	had	a pot.
Fog	was in	no ham.

1. A fox

2.

3

Language arts applications: story comprehension; writing sentences using words with the short sound of **o**

133

a e i **o** u

Examples

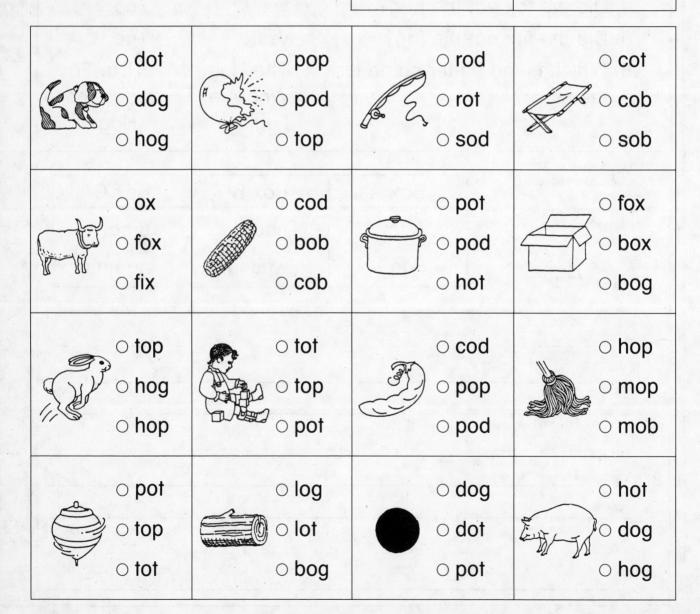

Directions: Say the name of the picture. Listen to the sound. Fill in the space next to the word that names the picture.

○ hop	○ fog
○ tot	○ fox
○ top	○ box

○ dot ○ dog ○ hog	○ pop ○ pod ○ top	○ rod ○ rot ○ sod	○ cot ○ cob ○ sob
○ ox ○ fox ○ fix	○ cod ○ bob ○ cob	○ pot ○ pod ○ hot	○ fox ○ box ○ bog
○ top ○ hog ○ hop	○ tot ○ top ○ pot	○ cod ○ pop ○ pod	○ hop ○ mop ○ mob
○ pot ○ top ○ tot	○ log ○ lot ○ bog	○ dog ○ dot ○ pot	○ hot ○ dog ○ hog

134

1 Say each picture name.
2 Listen for the short sound of **e**.
3 Color the picture if its name has the short sound of **e**.

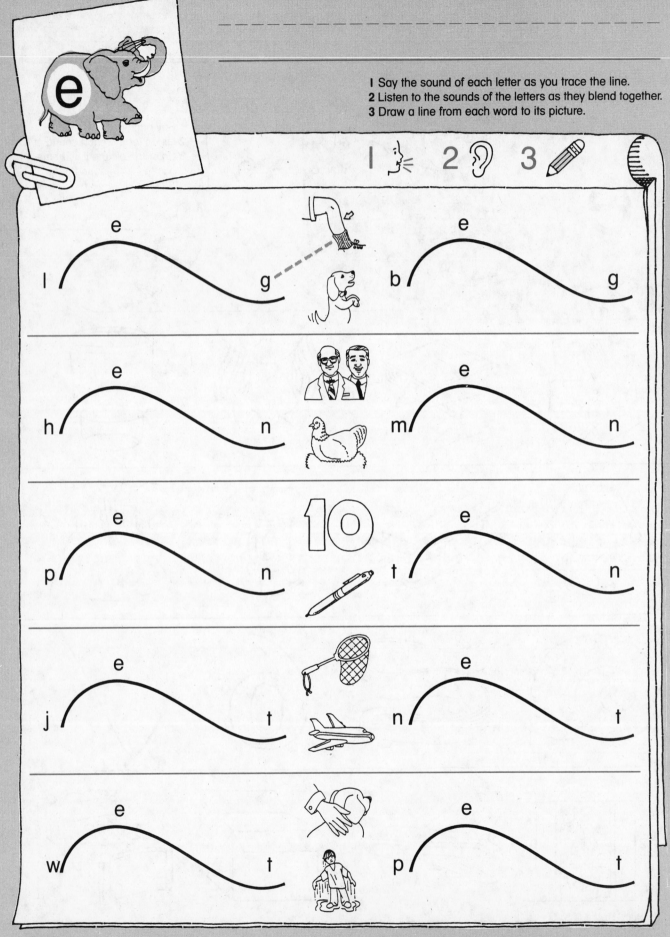

1 Say the sound of each letter as you trace the line.
2 Listen to the sounds of the letters as they blend together.
3 Draw a line from each word to its picture.

Using the short sound of **e**; blending words

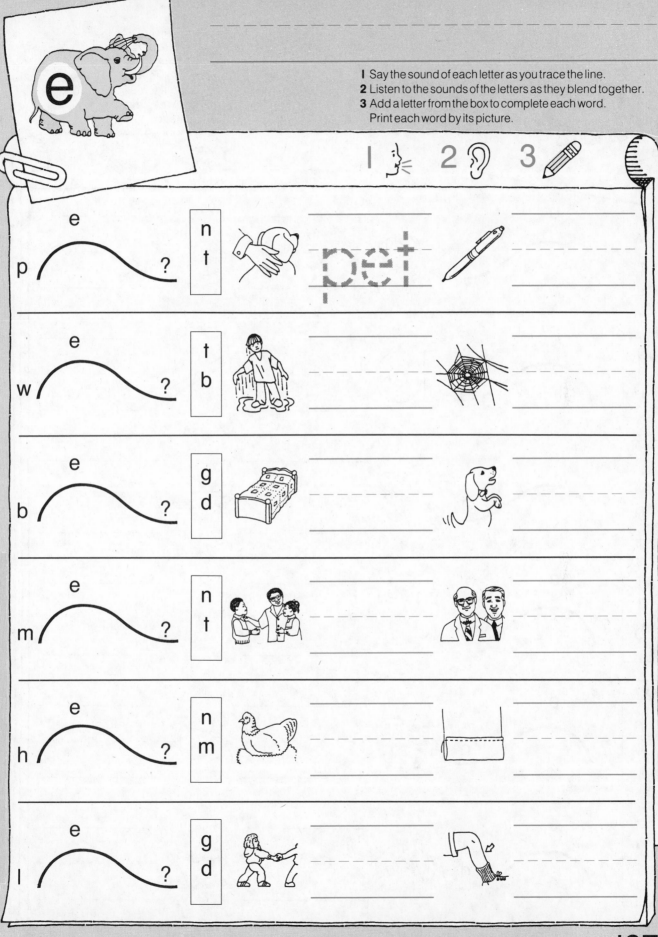

1 Say the sound of each letter as you trace the line.
2 Listen to the sounds of the letters as they blend together.
3 Add a letter from the box to complete each word.
   Print each word by its picture.

e
p ? | n t | pet

e
w ? | t b |

e
b ? | g d |

e
m ? | n t |

e
h ? | n m |

e
l ? | g d |

Using the short sound of **e**; blending words

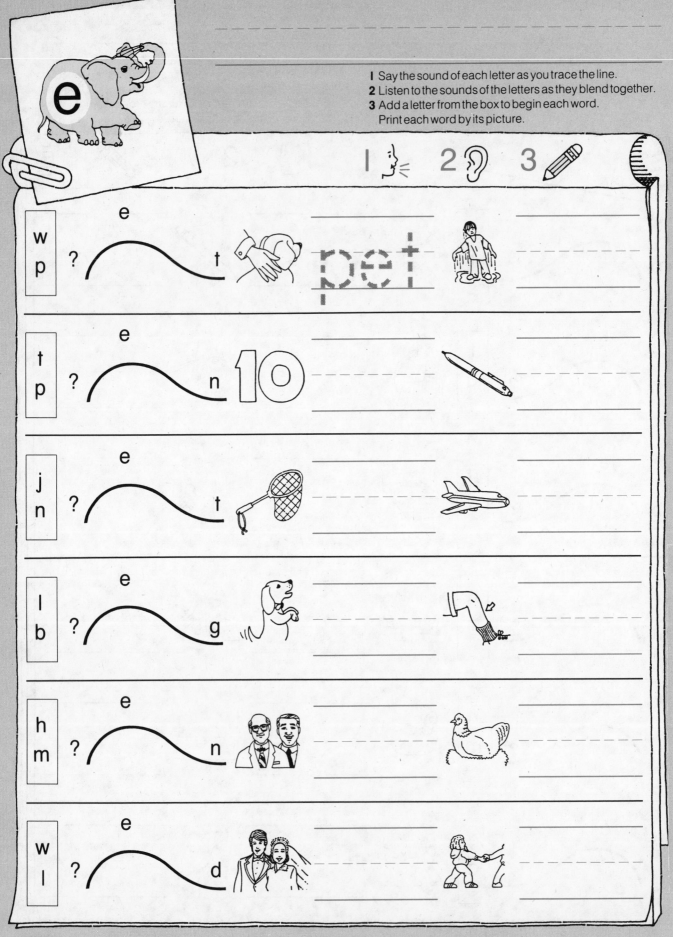

1 Say the sound of each letter as you trace the line.
2 Listen to the sounds of the letters as they blend together.
3 Add a letter from the box to begin each word.
Print each word by its picture.

1 2 3

w p	e ? ___ t	pet	
t p	e ? ___ n 10		
j n	e ? ___ t		
l b	e ? ___ g		
h m	e ? ___ n		
w l	e ? ___ d		

138

Using the short sound of **e**; blending words

1 Say each picture name.
2 Listen to the sound of each letter.
3 Print the word for the picture name.

1 2 3

hen

Using the short sound of **e**; spelling words

1 Say the two picture names in each box.
2 Listen to how they rhyme.
3 Print the picture names in the crossword puzzle.

1 🗣 2 👂 3 ✏️

beg   bed   men   pen   pet   ten

net   hen   jet   led   leg   wet

down ↓

1.

across →

2.

down ↓

1.

across →

2.

down ↓

1.

across →

2.

down ↓

1.

across →

2.

down ↓

1.

across →

2.

down ↓

1.

across →

2.

140

1 Read each sentence.
2 Fill in the space beside the word that makes sense in the sentence.
3 Print the word on the line.

1 📖 2 ✏️ 3 ✏️

Ten **men** will ___ a jet.
- ○ den
- ● men
- ○ met

Bev got the 🦋 ___ wet.
- ○ red
- ○ set
- ○ net

The dog can ___ for a 🦴 .
- ○ beg
- ○ bed
- ○ pen

Deb can pet the 🐴 in that ___ .
- ○ men
- ○ pen
- ○ jet

Ben has a 🦆 and a red ___ .
- ○ hem
- ○ get
- ○ hen

Ted hit his ___ on the 🚲 .
- ○ leg
- ○ met
- ○ let

Deb set the 🐶 on the ___ .
- ○ beg
- ○ led
- ○ bed

The ___ can set the 🐕 leg.
- ○ vet
- ○ bet
- ○ net

Language arts applications: using sentence context to select words with the short sound of **e**

1 Read each sentence.
2 Print the sentence that tells about the picture.

A pet sat on a mat.
A dog ran to the vet.

A pet sat on a mat.

Bev fed the pet at ten.
Bev set a net on a box.

Ben has a hen in his lap.
Ben has a pen in his bed.

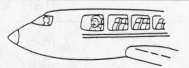

Ted can fit in the den.
Ted can sit in the jet.

The vet can get the hen.
The vet can pet a pig.

142

1 Read the story below. **2** Say each word.
3 Listen carefully for the short sound of **e**.
4 Draw a line under each word with the short sound of **e**.

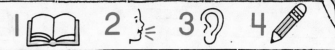

Ned had two hens in a pen.
Deb and Bev were red hens.

One day a big fox came to the pen.
It was about to get the hens.
Deb and Bev let out a yell.
"Help! Help! A fox is in the pen!"

Ned had a pet dog called Tex.
Ned said, "Get the fox out of the pen, Tex."

The fox had not met a dog like Tex.
That fox ran as if it had ten legs.
Yes, it went like a jet.

1 Read the story once more.
2 Then read the questions below.
3 Fill in the space by the correct answer.

1. Did Ned have ten hens? ○ yes ● no

2. Did a fox come to the pen? ○ yes ○ no

3. Did Deb and Bev yell for help? ○ yes ○ no

4. Did the fox get Deb and Bev? ○ yes ○ no

5. Will the fox get in the pen again? ○ yes ○ no

6. Which is the better name for the story? ○ The Fox and the Hens ○ Deb and Bev

---

1 Make up three sentences. Use words from boxes A, B, and C.
2 Print your sentences on the lines below.

  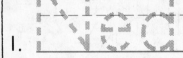

Box A	Box B	Box C
Ned	had	a red hen.
Bev	was	a dog.

1. _____

2. _____

3. _____

a $\boxed{e}$ i o u

Directions: Say the name of the picture. Listen to the sound. Fill in the space next to the word that names the picture.

Examples

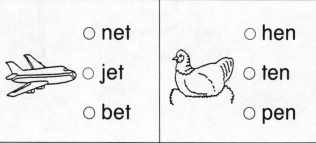

○ net	○ hen
○ jet	○ ten
○ bet	○ pen

10
○ pen
○ ten
○ den

○ wet
○ wed
○ web

○ pen
○ net
○ pet

○ met
○ men
○ get

○ beg
○ bed
○ bet

○ pen
○ ten
○ peg

○ leg
○ led
○ peg

○ wet
○ set
○ vet

○ net
○ set
○ get

○ leg
○ beg
○ bet

○ ten
○ net
○ set

○ led
○ bed
○ red

○ wed
○ web
○ beg

○ men
○ met
○ ten

○ web
○ wet
○ wed

○ let
○ get
○ pet

Testing the short sound of **e**; using an adapted standardized test format

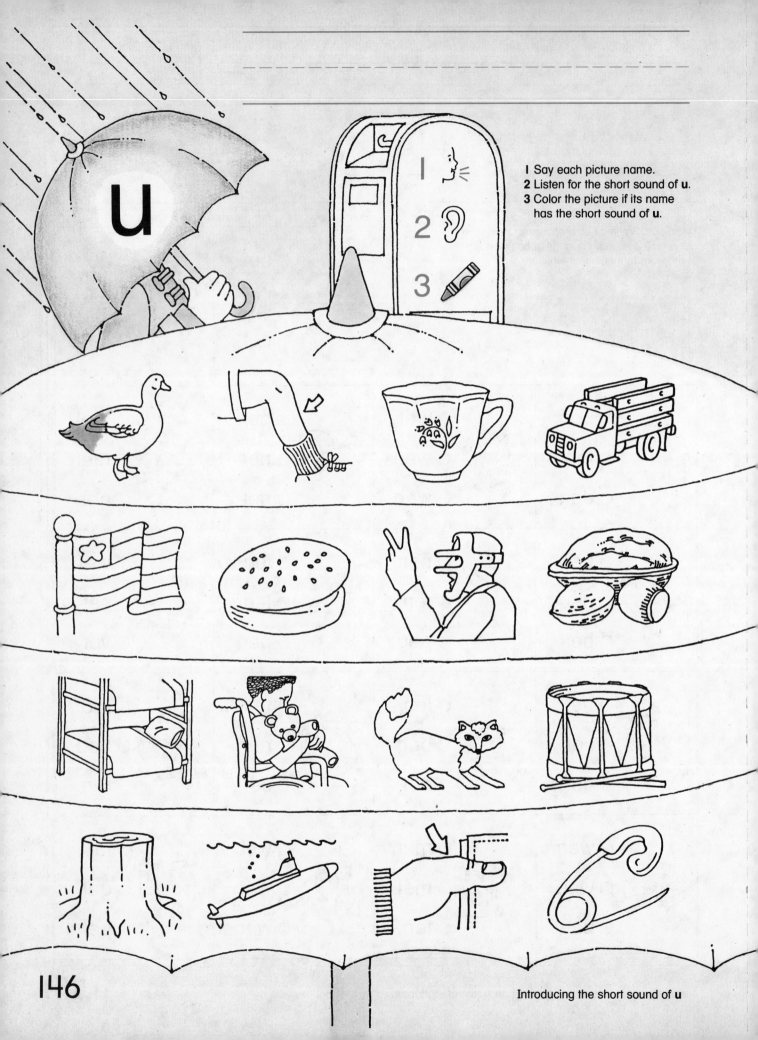

1 Say each picture name.
2 Listen for the short sound of **u**.
3 Color the picture if its name has the short sound of **u**.

Introducing the short sound of **u**

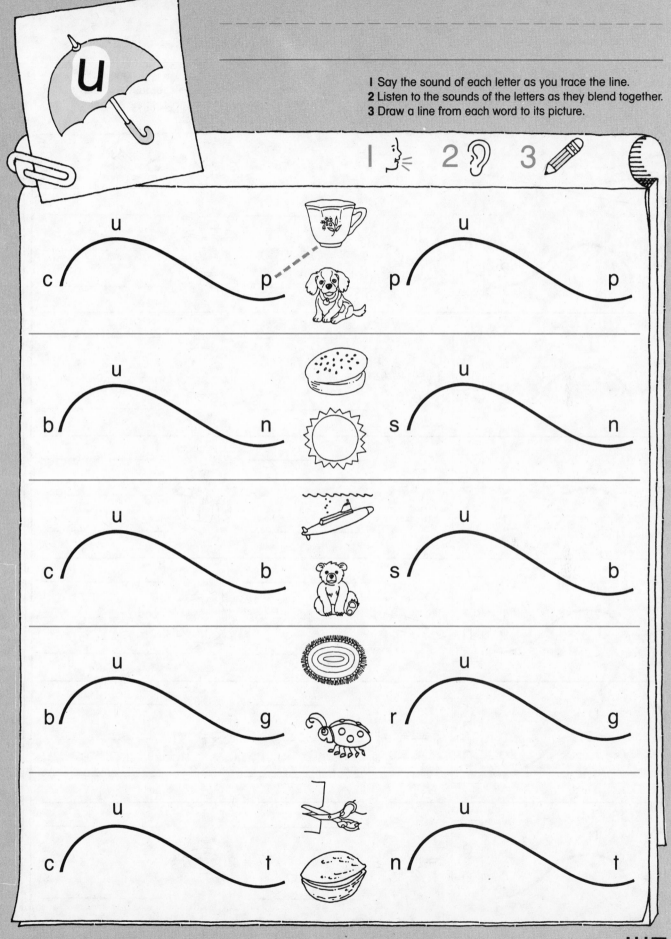

1 Say the sound of each letter as you trace the line.
2 Listen to the sounds of the letters as they blend together.
3 Draw a line from each word to its picture.

Using the short sound of **u**; blending words

147

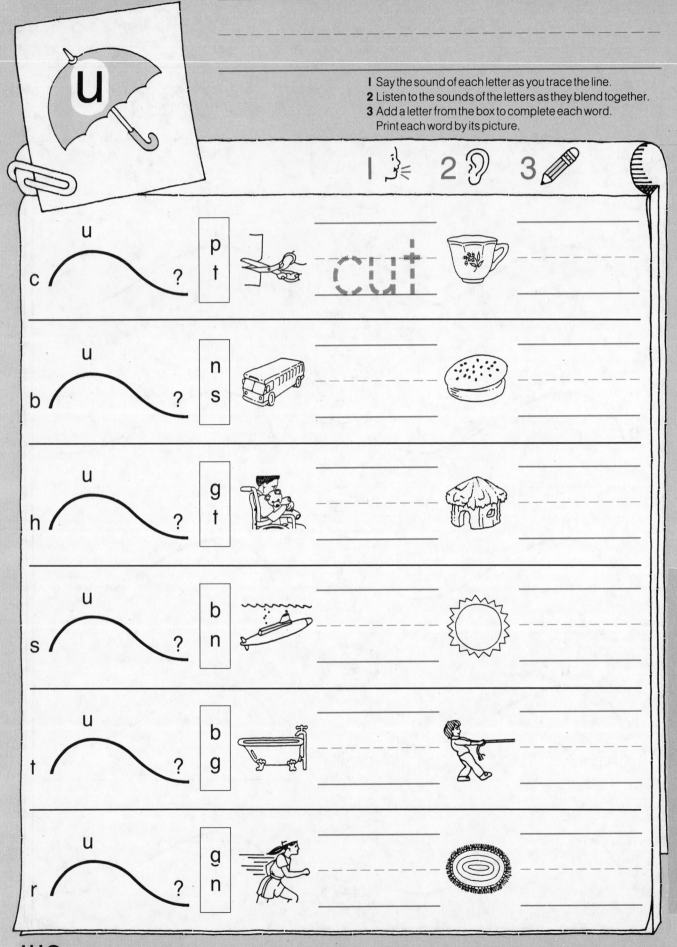

u

1 Say the sound of each letter as you trace the line.
2 Listen to the sounds of the letters as they blend together.
3 Add a letter from the box to complete each word.
  Print each word by its picture.

1 🗣 2 👂 3 ✏️

u
c   ? | p t | ✂️   cut

u
b   ? | n s |

u
h   ? | g t |

u
s   ? | b n |

u
t   ? | b g |

u
r   ? | g n |

Using the short sound of **u**; blending words

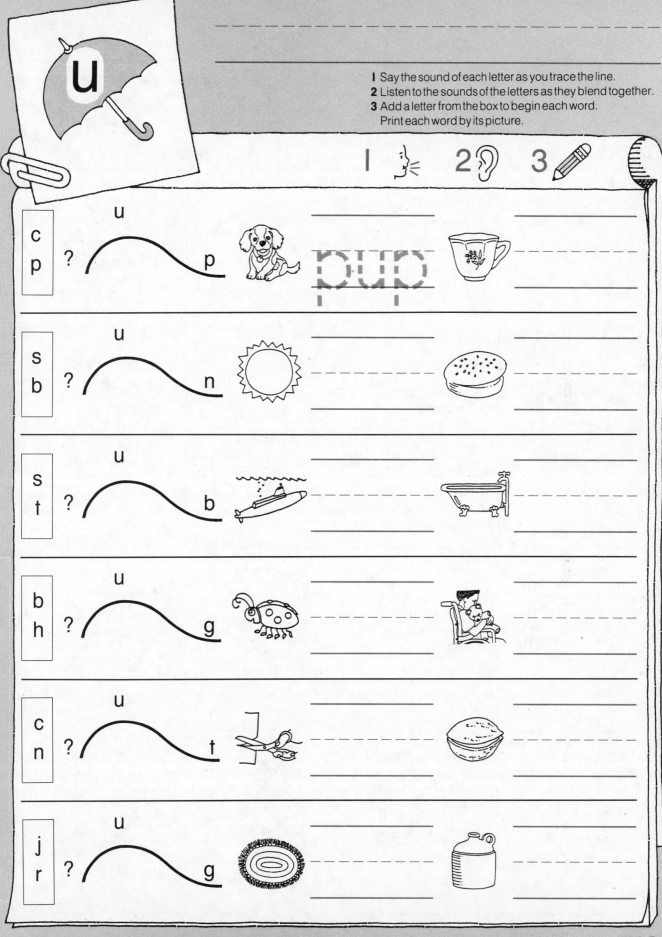

1 Say the sound of each letter as you trace the line.
2 Listen to the sounds of the letters as they blend together.
3 Add a letter from the box to begin each word.
   Print each word by its picture.

u

c p ? u p

s b ? u n

s t ? u b

b h ? u g

c n ? u t

j r ? u g

Using the short sound of **u**; blending words

1 Say each picture name.
2 Listen to the sound of each letter.
3 Print the word for the picture name.

cup

Using the short sound of **u**; spelling words

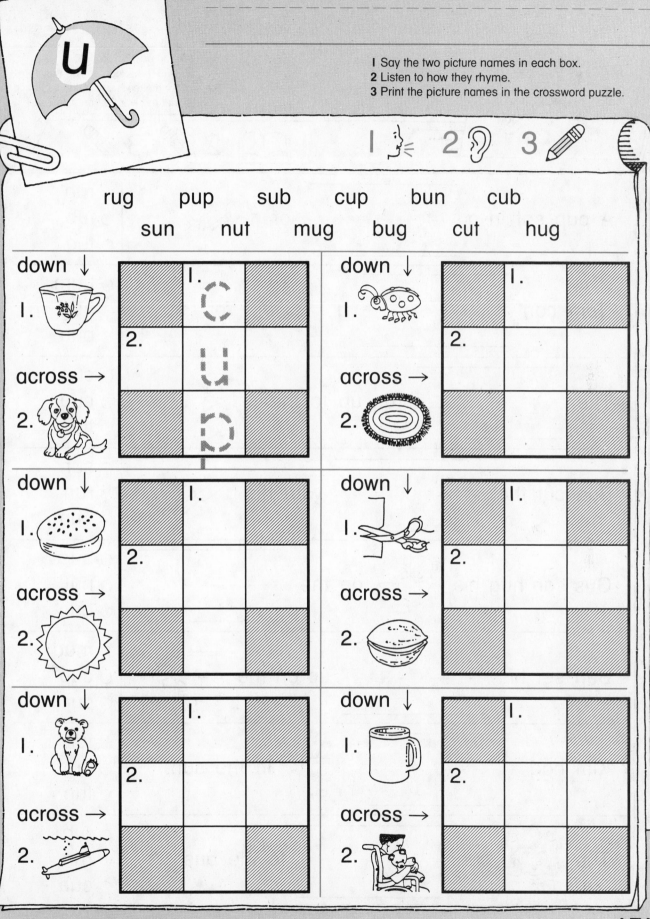

1 Say the two picture names in each box.
2 Listen to how they rhyme.
3 Print the picture names in the crossword puzzle.

rug   pup   sub   cup   bun   cub
sun   nut   mug   bug   cut   hug

down ↓
1.
across →
2.

down ↓
1.
across →
2.

down ↓
1.
across →
2.

down ↓
1.
across →
2.

down ↓
1.
across →
2.

down ↓
1.
across →
2.

Using the short sound of **u**; writing rhyming words

1 Read each sentence.
2 Fill in the space beside the word
   that makes sense in the sentence.
3 Print the word on the line.

u

A pup sat in a _tub_ of ⬙ .

- ○ rub
- ● tub
- ○ tug

Tom can _____ a 🎵 for us.

- ○ hum
- ○ hug
- ○ bug

The _____ ran up to the 🌳 .

- ○ cub
- ○ cup
- ○ tub

Bud cut the _____ with his 🔪 .

- ○ sun
- ○ run
- ○ bun

Gus can hug his 🧸 on the _____ .

- ○ bug
- ○ nut
- ○ bus

Ben set his _____ up on the 🪟 .

- ○ mud
- ○ cup
- ○ cut

Kim had _____ in the sun.

- ○ fun
- ○ bud
- ○ tub

The 👧 can _____ to the bus.

- ○ rub
- ○ run
- ○ cub

152

1 Read each sentence.
2 Print the sentence that tells about the picture.

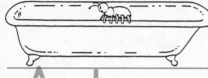

A bug sat on a rug.
A bug is on the tub.

A bug is on the tub.

The pup dug in the mud.
The cub had fun in the mud.

Al had fun in the sun.
Al has a pup on the bus.

The cub is on the rug.
The cub sat in the hut.

The mud is on the bus.
The mud is on the pup.

1 Read the story below. 2 Say each word.
3 Listen carefully for the short sound of **u**.
4 Draw a line under each word with the
   short sound of **u**.

A pup had run in the mud.

Bud got his pup out of the mud.

Then the pup gave a tug.

Bud saw it run on the rug.

He saw it jump on the bed.

"What a mess!" said Bud.

Bud made suds in a tub.

The pup had fun in the suds.

Bud took the pup out in the sun.

"I will rub you, little pup.

Then I will hug you.

Next time run in the sun.

Do not run in the mud."

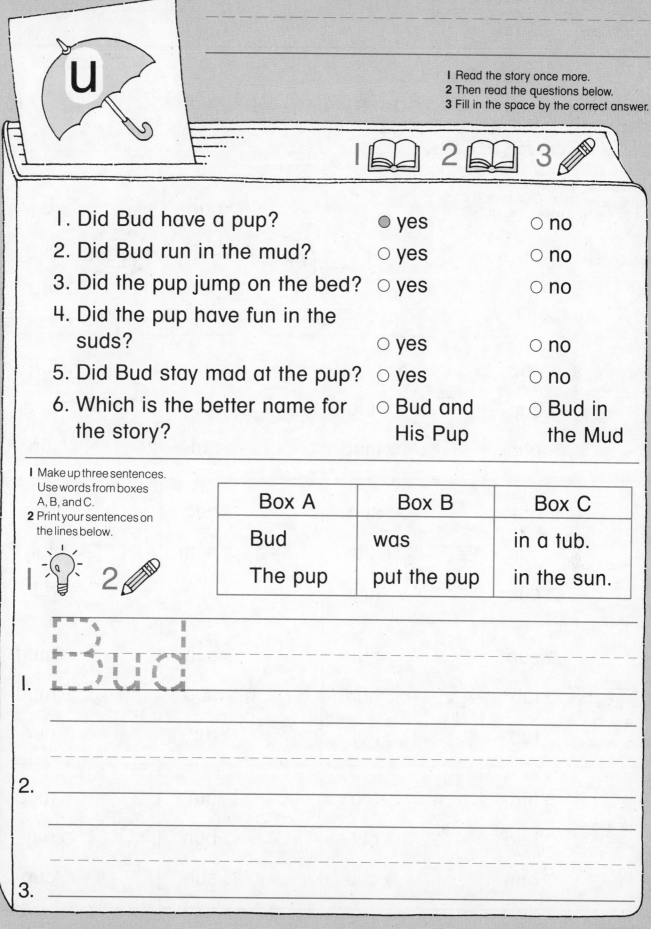

1 Read the story once more.
2 Then read the questions below.
3 Fill in the space by the correct answer.

1 🔖 2 📖 3 ✏️

1. Did Bud have a pup?   ● yes   ○ no
2. Did Bud run in the mud?   ○ yes   ○ no
3. Did the pup jump on the bed?   ○ yes   ○ no
4. Did the pup have fun in the suds?   ○ yes   ○ no
5. Did Bud stay mad at the pup?   ○ yes   ○ no
6. Which is the better name for the story?   ○ Bud and His Pup   ○ Bud in the Mud

1 Make up three sentences. Use words from boxes A, B, and C.
2 Print your sentences on the lines below.

💡 1   2 ✏️

Box A	Box B	Box C
Bud	was	in a tub.
The pup	put the pup	in the sun.

1. Bud

2.

3.

a e i o u

Examples

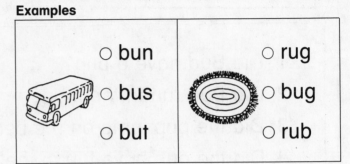

- ○ bun
- ○ bus
- ○ but

- ○ rug
- ○ bug
- ○ rub

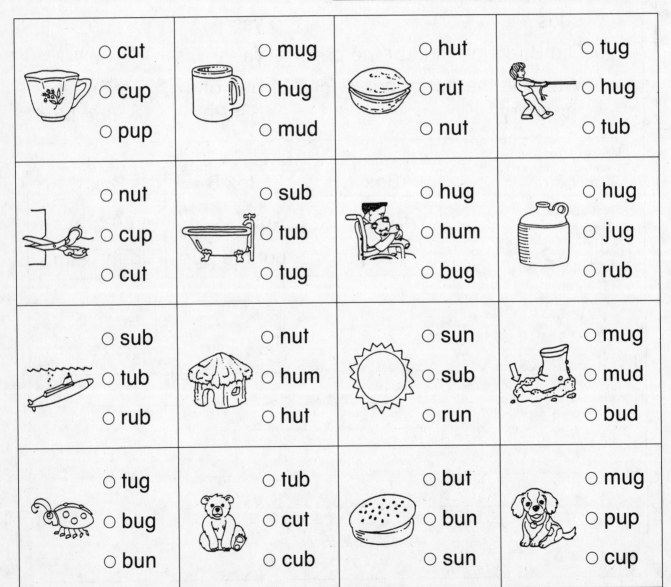

○ cut ○ cup ○ pup	○ mug ○ hug ○ mud	○ hut ○ rut ○ nut	○ tug ○ hug ○ tub
○ nut ○ cup ○ cut	○ sub ○ tub ○ tug	○ hug ○ hum ○ bug	○ hug ○ jug ○ rub
○ sub ○ tub ○ rub	○ nut ○ hum ○ hut	○ sun ○ sub ○ run	○ mug ○ mud ○ bud
○ tug ○ bug ○ bun	○ tub ○ cut ○ cub	○ but ○ bun ○ sun	○ mug ○ pup ○ cup

156

Testing the short sound of **u**; using an adapted standardized test format

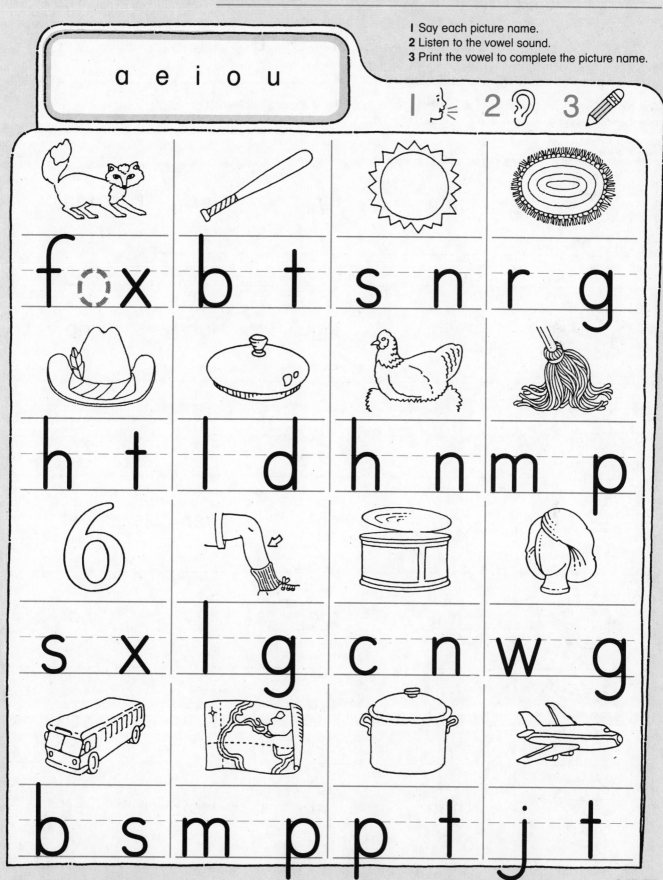

a e i o u

1   2   3

f o x   b t   s n   r g

h t   l d   h n   m p

6   s x   l g   c n   w g

b s   m p   p t   j t

Reviewing the short sounds of **a, e, i, o, u**

157

a e i o u

Directions: Say the name of the picture. Listen to the sound. Fill in the space below each word that has the same short vowel sound as the picture in the box.

Example

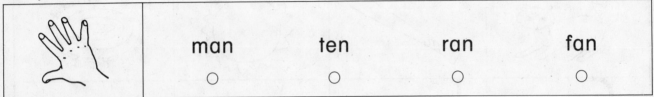

	man ○	ten ○	ran ○	fan ○
	wig ○	big ○	tub ○	rip ○
	pot ○	hit ○	not ○	cot ○
	pet ○	cot ○	web ○	net ○
	rag ○	rug ○	tub ○	hut ○
	pan ○	cap ○	can ○	cup ○
	hen ○	fin ○	wet ○	leg ○

Testing the short vowel sounds; using an adapted standardized test format

1 Say each picture name.
2 Listen for the long sound of **a**.
3 Color the picture if its name has the long sound of **a**.

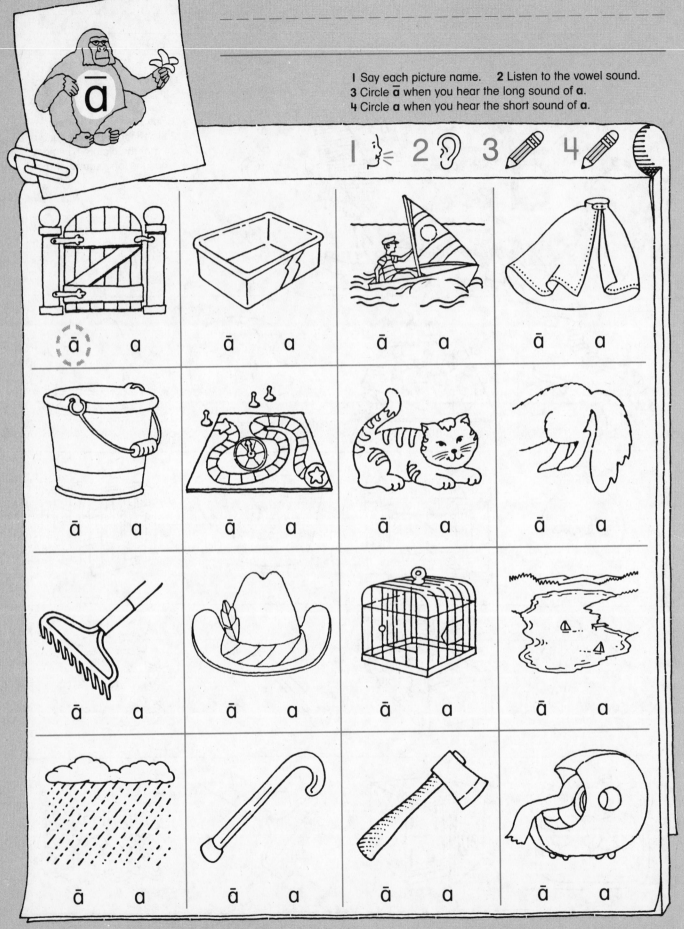

1 Say each picture name. 2 Listen to the vowel sound.
3 Circle ā when you hear the long sound of a.
4 Circle a when you hear the short sound of a.

160

1 Say each picture name.
2 Listen to the vowel sound.
3 Circle and then print the word for the picture name.

1 😮 2 👂 3 ✏️

ā

can + e = cāne

can (cane)	tap tape	van vane	pan pane
cane			
man mane	pan pane	cap cape	man mane
tap tape	van vane	cap cape	can cane

1 Say each picture name.
2 Listen to the vowel sound.
3 Circle and then print the word for the picture name.

pal + i = pā i̸l

bat (bait)	till tail	man main	rill rail
bait			
sill sail	mad maid	pal pail	ran rain
nil nail	pal pail	ran rain	mill mail

162

1 Say each picture name.
2 Listen to the vowel sound.
3 Circle and then print the word for the picture name.

1 👄 2 👂 3 ✏️

 = dāy

rag   (ray)

hat   hay

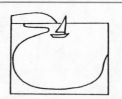
bag   bay

cap   Kay

ray

sad   say

man   may

wag   way

dam   day

nap   nay

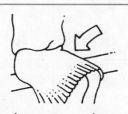
lap   lay

jam   jay

pan   pay

Using the long sound of **a**; spelling words

1 Say each picture name.   2 Listen for the long sound of **a**.
3 Circle the word for the picture name.
4 Mark the long sound of **a** and the silent letters as shown.

ā_e   āi   āy

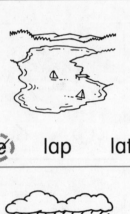		
(lāke) lap late	pail pane pal	hay ham hat
	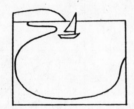	
ray ran rain	bay bat bake	make mane man

ray rag rake	gap gate game	sat save sail

dad dam date	mail made mat	dam day dad

164

Using the long sound of **a**

1 Say each picture name.
2 Listen for the long sound of **a**.
3 Print **a_e**, **ai** or **ay** when you hear the long sound of **a**.

1 2 3

a_e   ai   ay

t a p e l   l k   n   l h

p   l d   g m   m n

t   l r   k r   g t

b   m   l r   n c   n

1 Say each picture name.   2 Listen to the sound of each letter.
3 Print the word for the picture name. The letters in dark print
   show how to spell the long sound of **a** in each column.

a_e   **ai**   **ay**   **a_e**

lake

1 Say the two picture names in each box.
2 Listen to how they rhyme.
3 Print the picture names in the crossword puzzle.

1 🗣 2 👂 3 ✏️

pay rake hay pail lake sail rail nail

down ↓ 1. across → 2.

down ↓ 1. across → 2.

down ↓ 1. across → 2.

down ↓ 1. across → 2.

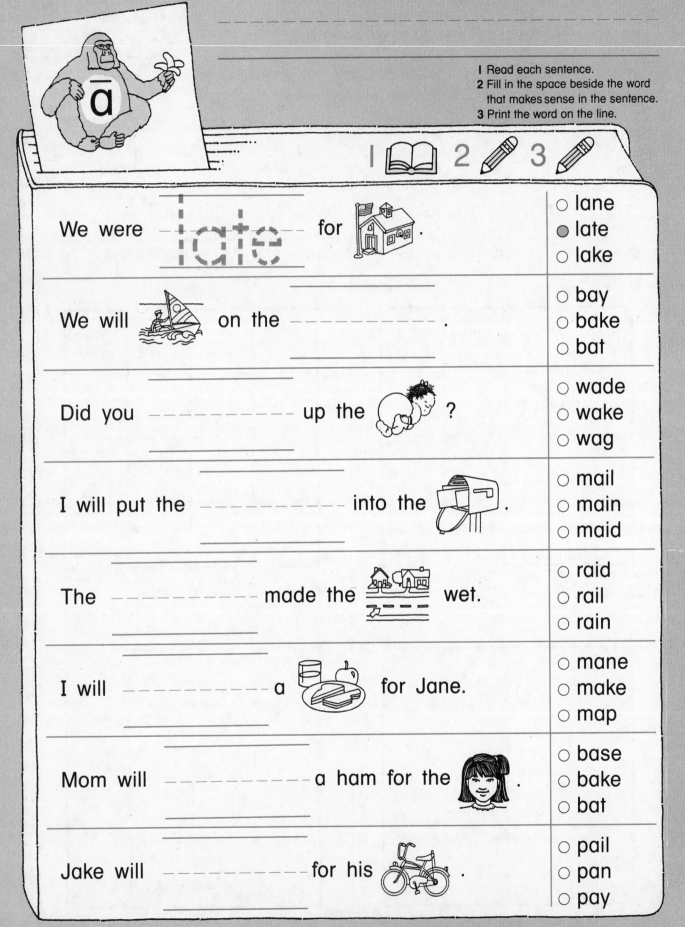

ā

1 Read each sentence.
2 Fill in the space beside the word that makes sense in the sentence.
3 Print the word on the line.

1 📖   2 ✏️   3 ✏️

We were **late** for .
- ○ lane
- ● late
- ○ lake

We will ⛵ on the _____ .
- ○ bay
- ○ bake
- ○ bat

Did you _____ up the ?
- ○ wade
- ○ wake
- ○ wag

I will put the _____ into the .
- ○ mail
- ○ main
- ○ maid

The _____ made the wet.
- ○ raid
- ○ rail
- ○ rain

I will _____ a for Jane.
- ○ mane
- ○ make
- ○ map

Mom will _____ a ham for the .
- ○ base
- ○ bake
- ○ bat

Jake will _____ for his .
- ○ pail
- ○ pan
- ○ pay

168

Language arts applications: using sentence context to select words with the long sound of **a**

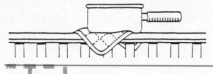

The pan is on a rail.
The pane has a rail.

The pan is on a rail.

Dave put a rake by the lake.
The rake is by a gate.

The pane has a cape.
Mai put tape on a pane.

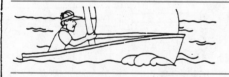

Jay will sail in the rain.
Jay set sail on a lake.

Kay will rake the hay.
Kay will make a hat.

1 Read the story below. 2 Say each word.
3 Listen carefully for the long sound of **a**.
4 Draw a line under each word with the long sound of **a**.

Jake likes to bake. One day, he made
a date cake. Then he ran out to play.

Jake has a dog. His name is Nate.
Nate came up to the cake.
He gave his tail a wag.
Then he ate the cake.

Jake came in from play. He gave a wail.
"My cake! Where is my cake?"

Nate gave his tail a wag. Jake looked at Nate.
Jake said, "I see who ate my cake."

170

Language arts applications: reading a story with words with the long sound of **a**

1 Read the story once more.
2 Then read the questions below.
3 Fill in the space by the correct answer.

1. Did Nate bake a cake? ○ yes ● no

2. Did Jake have a dog? ○ yes ○ no

3. Did Jake wag his tail? ○ yes ○ no

4. Did Nate eat the cake? ○ yes ○ no

5. Will Jake hug Nate? ○ yes ○ no

6. Which is the better name for the story? ○ Jake Has a Dog ○ Nate Eats a Cake

1 Make up three sentences. Use words from boxes A, B, and C.
2 Print your sentences on the lines below.

Box A	Box B	Box C
Nate	likes	Jake.
Jake	baked a	cake.

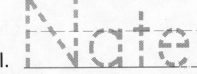

1. Nate

2.

3.

Language arts applications: story comprehension; writing sentences using words with the long sound of **a**

171

ā ē ī ō ū

Directions: Say the name of the picture. Listen to the sound. Fill in the space next to the word that names the picture.

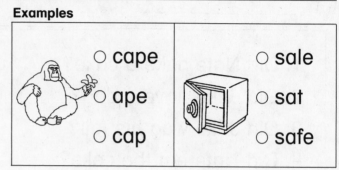

○ cape   ○ sale
○ ape   ○ sat
○ cap   ○ safe

○ came ○ cane ○ can	○ safe ○ sail ○ sat	○ nail ○ nap ○ name	○ hat ○ hail ○ hay
○ late ○ lap ○ lake	○ mane ○ make ○ man	○ ran ○ rail ○ rain	○ day ○ date ○ dam
○ cape ○ cap ○ cane	○ pan ○ pane ○ pail	○ dad ○ dale ○ date	○ main ○ mail ○ mill
○ gas ○ gate ○ game	○ rake ○ ran ○ rain	○ bale ○ bay ○ bat	○ tap ○ tale ○ tape

Testing the long sound of **a**; using an adapted standardized test format

1 Say each picture name.
2 Listen for the long sound of **i**.
3 Color the picture if its name has the long sound of **i**.

Introducing the long sound of **i**

1 Say each picture name. 2 Listen to the vowel sound.
3 Circle ī when you hear the long sound of i.
4 Circle i when you hear the short sound of i.

174

1 Say each picture name.
2 Listen to the vowel sound.
3 Circle and then print the word for the picture name.

pin + e = pine

pin (pine)	dim dime	kit kite	pill pile
pine			
rid ride	fir fire	fill file	kit kite
fill file	fin fine	bit bite	pin pine

1 Say each picture name.   2 Listen for the long sound of **i**.
3 Circle the word for the picture name.
4 Mark the long sound of **i** and the silent letter as shown.

ī_e

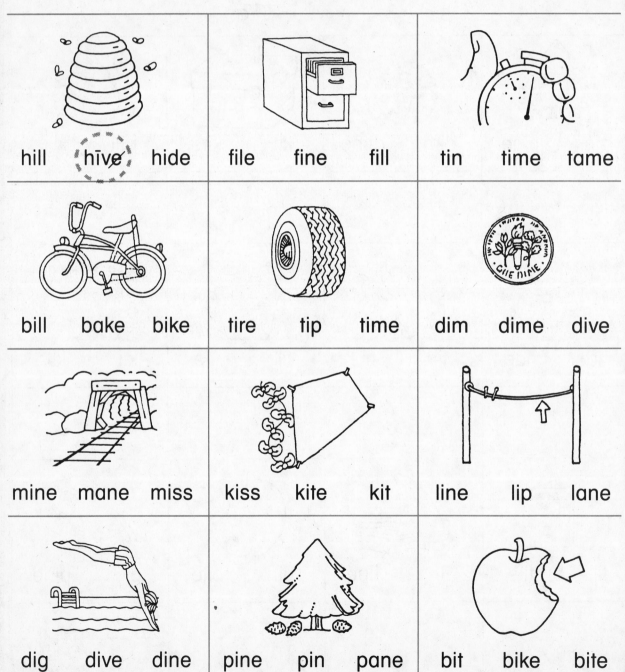

hill (hīve) hide	file fine fill	tin time tame
bill bake bike	tire tip time	dim dime dive
mine mane miss	kiss kite kit	line lip lane
dig dive dine	pine pin pane	bit bike bite

176

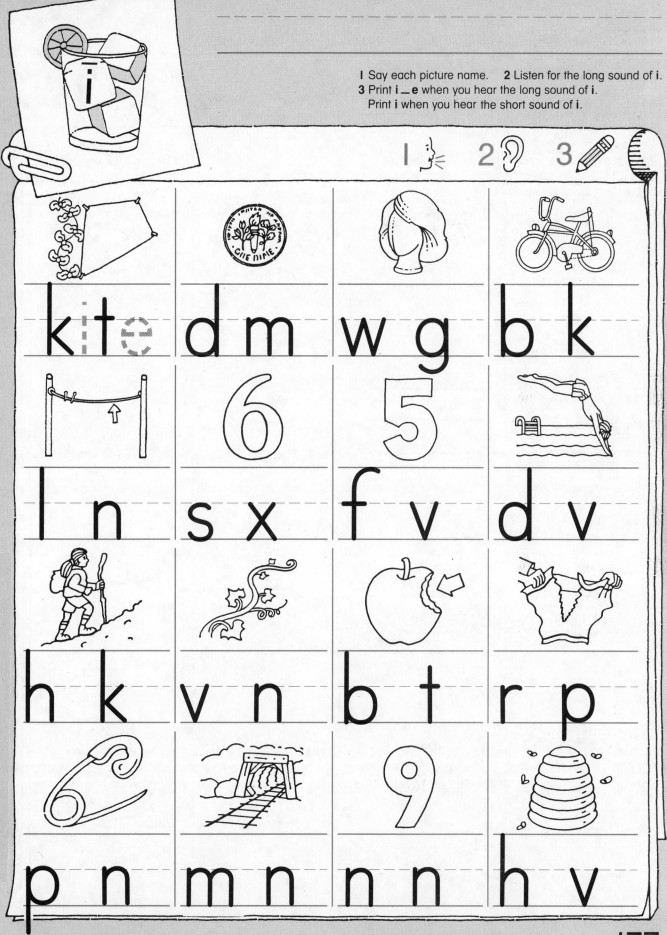

1 Say each picture name.   2 Listen for the long sound of i.
3 Print i __ e when you hear the long sound of i.
   Print i when you hear the short sound of i.

1 🗣   2 👂   3 ✏️

k i t e   d m   w g   b k

l n   6   5

s x   f v   d v

h k   v n   b t   r p

p n   m n   n n   h v

1 Say each picture name.
2 Listen to the sound of each letter.
3 Print the word for the picture name.

nine

Using the long sound of **i**; spelling words

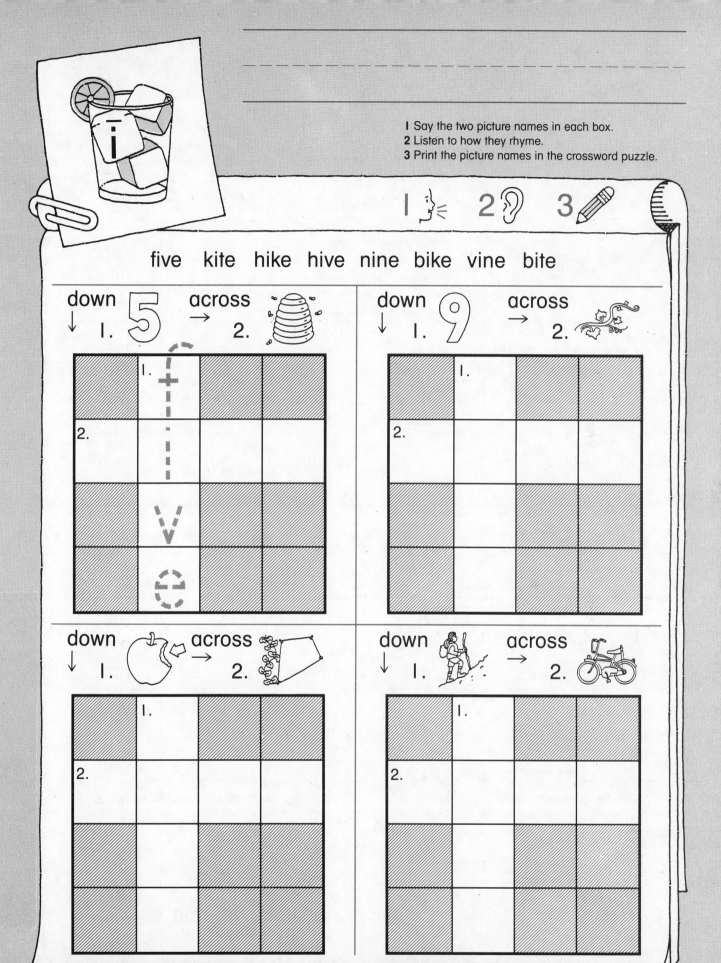

1 Say the two picture names in each box.
2 Listen to how they rhyme.
3 Print the picture names in the crossword puzzle.

five   kite   hike   hive   nine   bike   vine   bite

Using the long sound of **i**; writing rhyming words

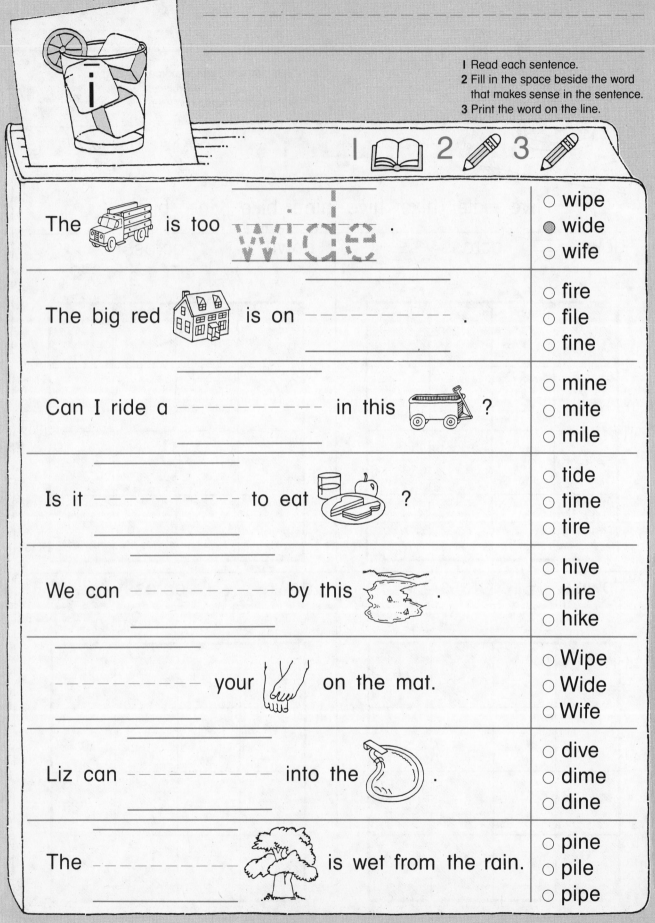

1 Read each sentence.
2 Fill in the space beside the word that makes sense in the sentence.
3 Print the word on the line.

1 📖 2 ✏️ 3 ✏️

The 🚚 is too **wide** .

- ○ wipe
- ● wide
- ○ wife

The big red 🏠 is on _____ .

- ○ fire
- ○ file
- ○ fine

Can I ride a _____ in this 🛒 ?

- ○ mine
- ○ mite
- ○ mile

Is it _____ to eat 🍽️ ?

- ○ tide
- ○ time
- ○ tire

We can _____ by this 🏞️ .

- ○ hive
- ○ hire
- ○ hike

_____ your ✋ on the mat.

- ○ Wipe
- ○ Wide
- ○ Wife

Liz can _____ into the ⭕ .

- ○ dive
- ○ dime
- ○ dine

The _____ 🌳 is wet from the rain.

- ○ pine
- ○ pile
- ○ pipe

Language arts applications: using sentence context to select words with the long sound of **i**

 1 2

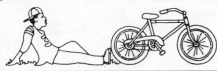

Mom has a fine vine.
Mike has a fine bike.

Mike has a fine bike

Jane will hike for a mile.
Jake will hide by a hive.

Kit can ride on a kite.
Kit can fix that kite.

Five dimes are in a pile.
Six limes are in a pile.

Lil can ride on a wire.
Lil can dive off a wire.

Language arts applications: using the long sound of **i** to select sentences from context

1 Read the story below.   **2** Say each word.
3 Listen carefully for the long sound of **i**.
4 Draw a line under each word with the
   long sound of **i**.

Kit likes to hike. Mike likes to bike.

Kit hikes to the top of Pine Hill.

Mike takes his bike.

Then they sit under a pine to eat.

Mike says, "I like to bike and hike.

You can ride my bike down the hill."

Kit says, "Fine. I like to hike.

Then I like to ride a bike."

Language arts applications: reading a story with words with the long sound of **i**

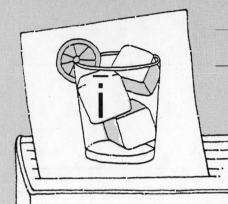

1 Read the story once more.
2 Then read the questions below.
3 Fill in the space by the correct answer.

1 📖 2 📖 3 ✏️

1. Did Mike and Kit go up Pine Hill? ● yes ○ no
2. Did they hike to Pine Lake? ○ yes ○ no
3. Did they sit under a pine? ○ yes ○ no
4. Will Kit ride the bike? ○ yes ○ no
5. Did they have a fine time? ○ yes ○ no
6. Which is the better name for the story? ○ Mike and Kit Go to Pine Hill ○ Mike Sits Under a Pine

1 Make up three sentences. Use words from boxes A, B, and C.
2 Print your sentences on the lines below.

 1 💡 2 ✏️

Box A	Box B	Box C
Mike	can take	the bike.
Kit	can ride	a hike.

1.

2.

3.

ā ē ī̄ ō ū

Directions: Say the name of the picture. Listen to the sound. Fill in the space next to the word that names the picture.

Examples

○ pail	○ pill
○ pit	○ pile
○ pipe	○ pal

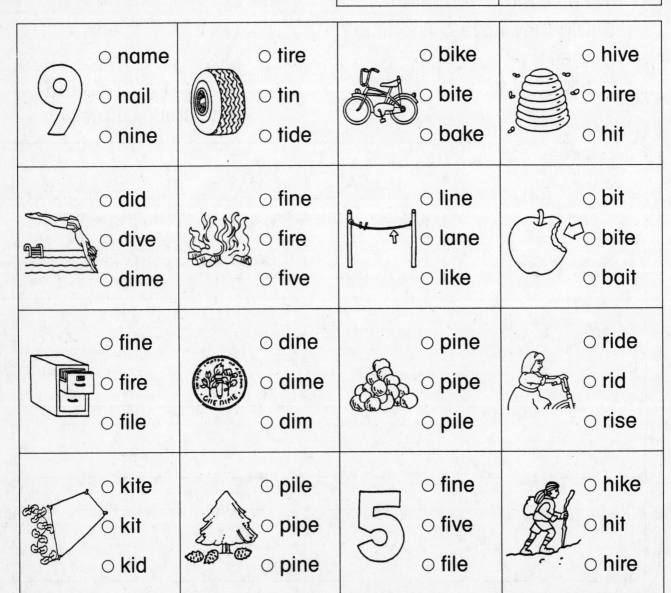

○ name ○ nail ○ nine	○ tire ○ tin ○ tide	○ bike ○ bite ○ bake	○ hive ○ hire ○ hit
○ did ○ dive ○ dime	○ fine ○ fire ○ five	○ line ○ lane ○ like	○ bit ○ bite ○ bait
○ fine ○ fire ○ file	○ dine ○ dime ○ dim	○ pine ○ pipe ○ pile	○ ride ○ rid ○ rise
○ kite ○ kit ○ kid	○ pile ○ pipe ○ pine	○ fine ○ five ○ file	○ hike ○ hit ○ hire

Testing the long sound of **i**; using an adapted standardized test format

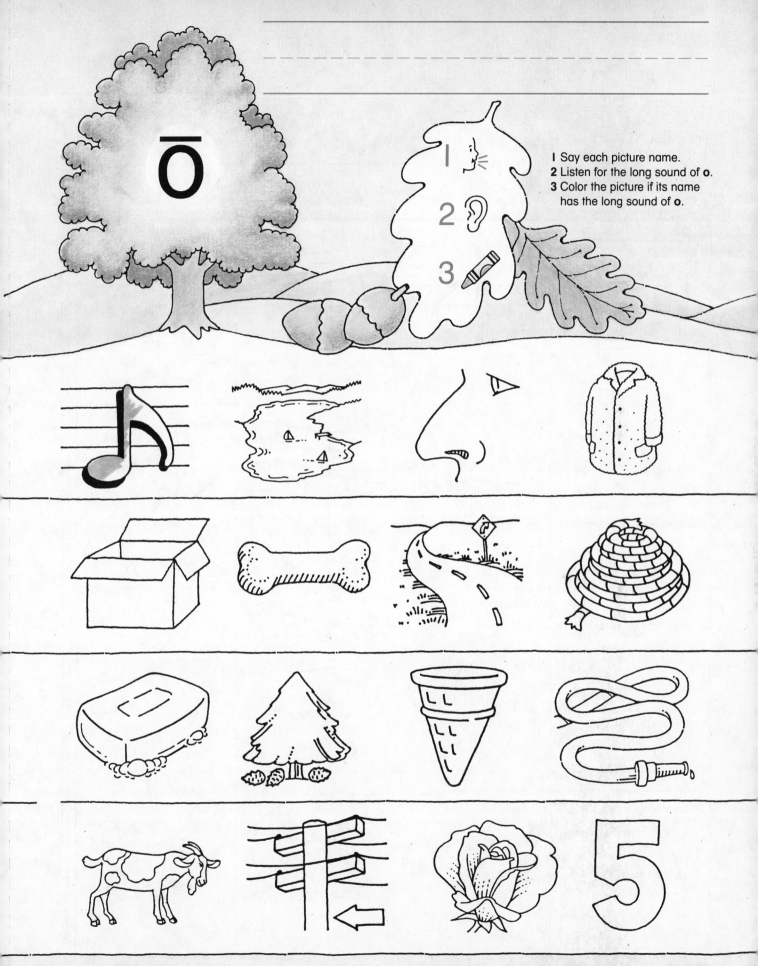

Ō

1 Say each picture name.
2 Listen for the long sound of **o**.
3 Color the picture if its name has the long sound of **o**.

ō

1 Say each picture name.   **2** Listen to the vowel sound.
3 Circle **ō** when you hear the long sound of **o**.
4 Circle **o** when you hear the short sound of **o**.

1   2   3   4

ō   o   ō   o   ō   o   ō   o

ō   o   ō   o   ō   o   ō   o

ō   o   ō   o   ō   o   ō   o

ō   o   ō   o   ō   o   ō   o

186

1 Say each picture name.
2 Listen to the vowel sound.
3 Circle and then print the word for the picture name.

1 🗣 2 👂 3 ✏️

cod + e = 🖂 cōde

con   (cone)   Rob   robe   not   note   tot   tote

cone

cod   code   hop   hope   mop   mope   cod   code

Sol   sole   rod   rode   Ross   rose   dot   dote

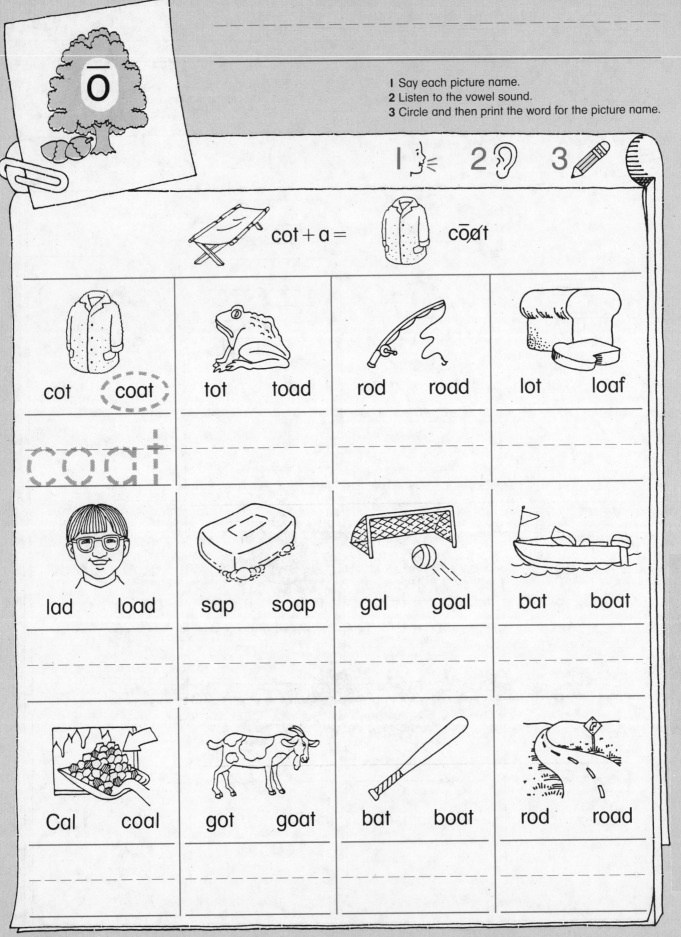

ō

1 Say each picture name.
2 Listen to the vowel sound.
3 Circle and then print the word for the picture name.

1 | 2 | 3

cot + a =   cōat

cot (coat)	tot toad	rod road	lot loaf
coat			
lad load	sap soap	gal goal	bat boat
Cal coal	got goat	bat boat	rod road

188

Using the long sound of **o**; spelling words

$\bar{o}$

1 Say each picture name. 2 Listen for the long sound of **o**.
3 Circle the word for the picture name.
4 Mark the long sound of **o** and the silent letters as shown.

1 🗣 2 👂 3 ✏ 4 ✏

ō_e̸ ōa̸

(hōme) hop hope	rob rode robe	soak side sad
goat got gate	cot cove cone	bone box boat
rot rose rise	file fog foal	rope rob role
late toad tot	note mole not	cot cape coat

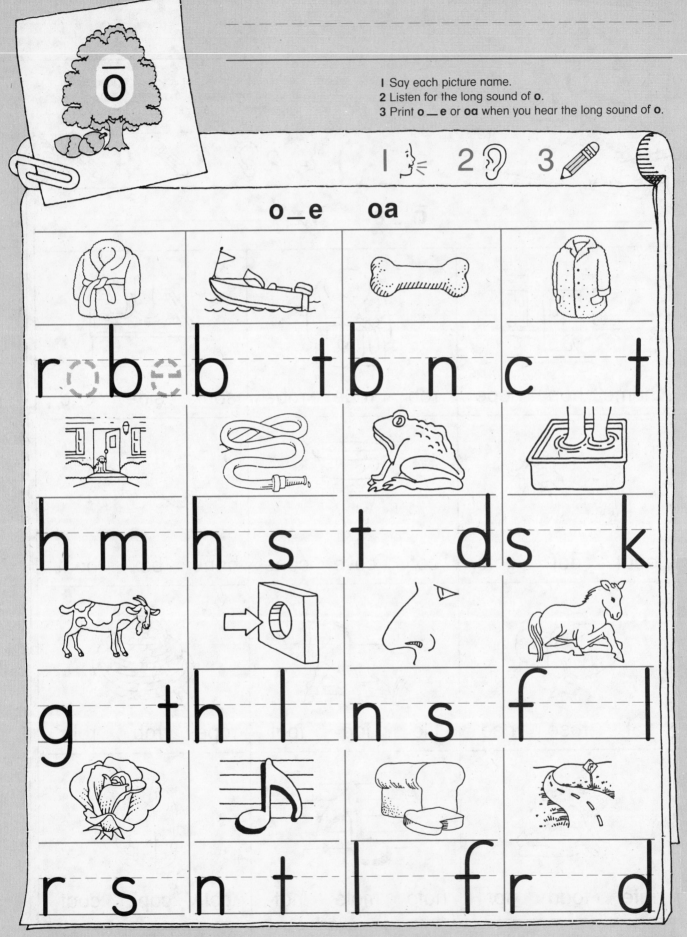

1 Say each picture name.
2 Listen for the long sound of **o**.
3 Print **o ＿ e** or **oa** when you hear the long sound of **o**.

1 2 3

o＿e   oa

r o b e b   t b n   c t

h m   h s t   d s   k

g   t h l   n s   f l

r s   n t l   f r   d

Using the long sound of **o**

1 Say each picture name.   2 Listen to the sound of each letter.
3 Print the word for the picture name. The letters in dark print
show how to spell the long sound of **o** in each column.

1   2   3

o_e	oa	o_e	oa
rose			

Using the long sound of **o**; spelling words

191

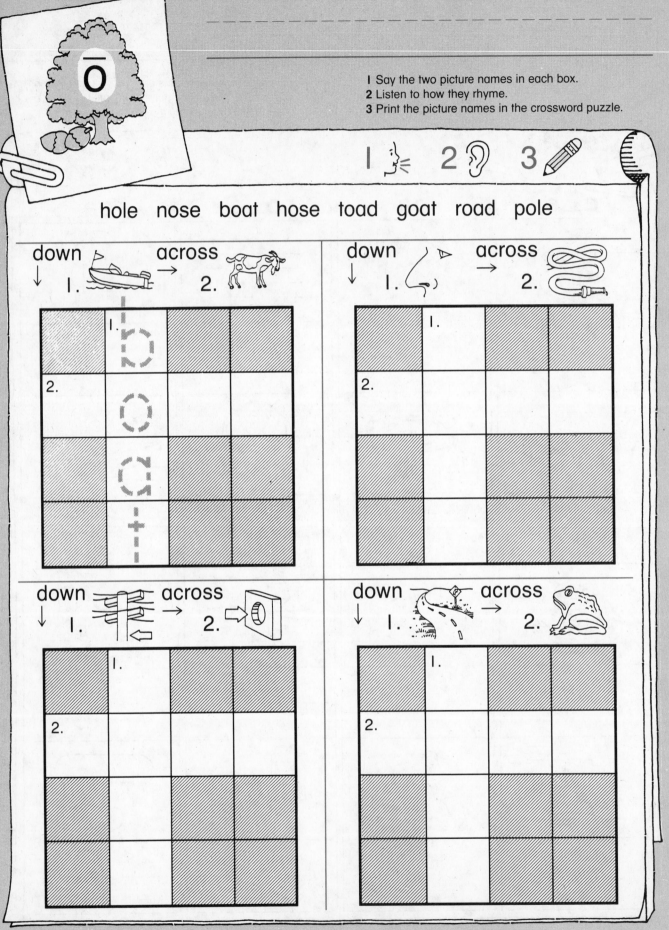

1 Say the two picture names in each box.
2 Listen to how they rhyme.
3 Print the picture names in the crossword puzzle.

hole   nose   boat   hose   toad   goat   road   pole

down → 1.   across → 2.

down → 1.   across → 2.

down → 1.   across → 2.

down → 1.   across → 2.

192

Using the long sound of **o**; writing rhyming words

ō

1 Read each sentence.
2 Fill in the space beside the word that makes sense in the sentence.
3 Print the word on the line.

1 📖 2 ✏️ 3 ✏️

I will ✉️ a note to my dad.

- ● note
- ○ not
- ○ nose

I paid five 💵 for that _____ .

- ○ hole
- ○ hose
- ○ hope

Do not get _____ in your 👁️ 👁️ .

- ○ soak
- ○ sop
- ○ soap

Mom will bake the _____ in the 🔥 .

- ○ loan
- ○ loaf
- ○ load

I will 👉 my _____ with the hose.

- ○ rose
- ○ rode
- ○ rope

Joan put her _____ in the 🚪 .

- ○ coat
- ○ cot
- ○ coal

The _____ ate our 🌸 .

- ○ got
- ○ goat
- ○ goal

I _____ I will get a 📄 .

- ○ home
- ○ hope
- ○ hop

Language arts applications: using sentence context to select words with the long sound of **o**

193

$\bar{o}$

The boat has a pole.
The boat has a hole.

The boat has a pole.

He has a rose on his coat.
He gave a rose to Joan.

Joan got a note.
The note is in her coat.

A toad is in the road.
A coat is in the road.

A rope is in the hole.
A mole is in the hole.

Ō

1 Read the story below.   2 Say each word.
3 Listen carefully for the long sound of **o**.
4 Draw a line under each word with the
  long sound of **o**.

Joe has a goat named Rose.

One day, Rose ate a hole in a coat.

Then she ate a hole in a box of soap.

Joe yelled at Rose.

"Stop! Soap is not for a goat."

Joe got a rope to tie his goat to a pole.

He got a load of oats for Rose.

He said, "Oats are what goats

like to eat."

Rose said, "Naa, naa, naa."

Language arts applications: reading a story with words with the long sound of **o**

$\bar{o}$

1 Read the story once more.
2 Then read the questions below.
3 Fill in the space by the correct answer.

1 📖 2 📖 3 ✏️

1. Did Joe have a goat?   ● yes   ○ no
2. Is the goat named Rose?   ○ yes   ○ no
3. Did the goat bite Joe?   ○ yes   ○ no
4. Did Joe rope the goat?   ○ yes   ○ no
5. Will the goat stay by the pole? ○ yes   ○ no
6. Which is the better name for   ○ A Goat   ○ Rose
   the story?   in the Road   and the
                                                    Oats

1 Make up three sentences.
Use words from boxes
A, B, and C.
2 Print your sentences on
the lines below.

 1 2 ✏️

Box A	Box B	Box C
Rose	had	oats.
Joe	ate	a goat.

1. Rose _____

2. _____

3. _____

196   Language arts applications: story comprehension; writing sentences using words with the long sound of o

ā ē ī ō̄ ū

Directions: Say the name of the picture.
Listen to the sound. Fill in the space next
to the word that names the picture.

Examples

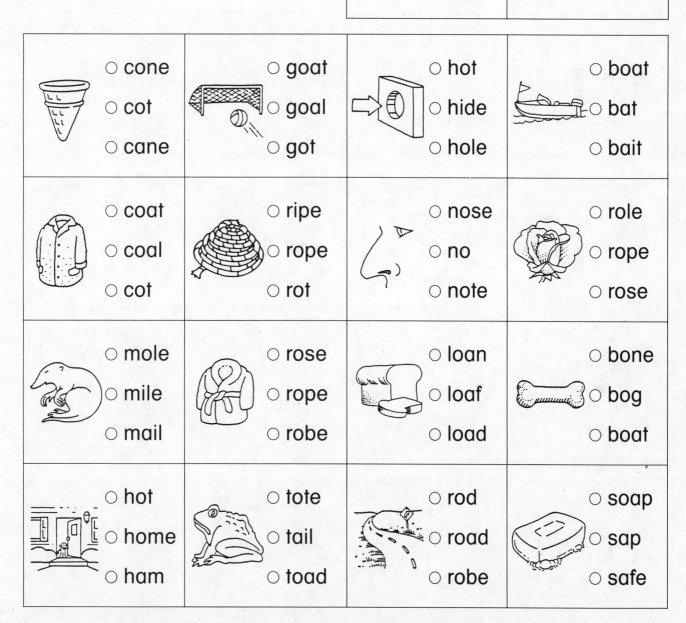

○ fail	○ hole
○ foal	○ hot
○ fog	○ hose

○ cone	○ goat	○ hot	○ boat
○ cot	○ goal	○ hide	○ bat
○ cane	○ got	○ hole	○ bait
○ coat	○ ripe	○ nose	○ role
○ coal	○ rope	○ no	○ rope
○ cot	○ rot	○ note	○ rose
○ mole	○ rose	○ loan	○ bone
○ mile	○ rope	○ loaf	○ bog
○ mail	○ robe	○ load	○ boat
○ hot	○ tote	○ rod	○ soap
○ home	○ tail	○ road	○ sap
○ ham	○ toad	○ robe	○ safe

Testing the long sound of **o**; using an adapted standardized test format

1 Say each picture name.
2 Listen for the long sound of **e**.
3 Color the picture if its name has the long sound of **e**.

Introducing the long sound of **e**

1 Say each picture name.   2 Listen to the vowel sound.
3 Circle ē when you hear the long sound of e.
4 Circle e when you hear the short sound of e.

1 ⟨ 2 ⟩ 3 ✏ 4 ✏

ē e   ē e   ē e   ē e

ē e   ē e   ē e   ē e

ē e   ē e   ē e   ē e

ē e   ē e   ē e   ē e

Using the long sound of **e**

199

1 Say each picture name.
2 Listen to the vowel sound.
3 Circle and then print the word for the picture name.

bed + a = bēad

met (meat)   pass   peas   bed   bead   pet   peat

meat

net   neat   red   read   Ben   bean   sell   seal

bed   bead   set   seat   Mel   meal   men   mean

200

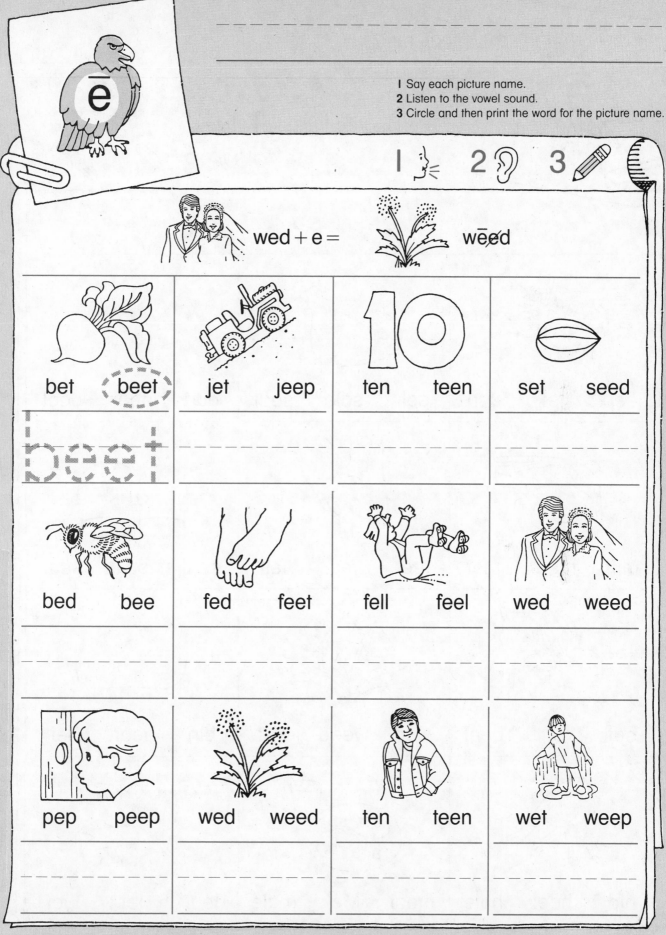

1 Say each picture name.
2 Listen to the vowel sound.
3 Circle and then print the word for the picture name.

1 🗣 2 👂 3 ✏️

wed + e = wēēd

bet ⬭beet⬭	jet jeep	ten teen	set seed
beet			
bed bee	fed feet	fell feel	wed weed
pep peep	wed weed	ten teen	wet weep

ē

1 Say each picture name.   2 Listen for the long sound of **e**.
3 Circle the word for the picture name.
4 Mark the long sound of **e** and the silent letters as shown.

1 🗣   2 👂   3 ✏   4 ✏

ēe   ēa

(jēep) jet Jan	sell sale seal	dad deer deal
mitt meat met	feet fed fell	seat sell seal
bat bit beet	wed weed wet	bin bean Ben
hid heel hole	meal Mel male	leaf let loaf

202

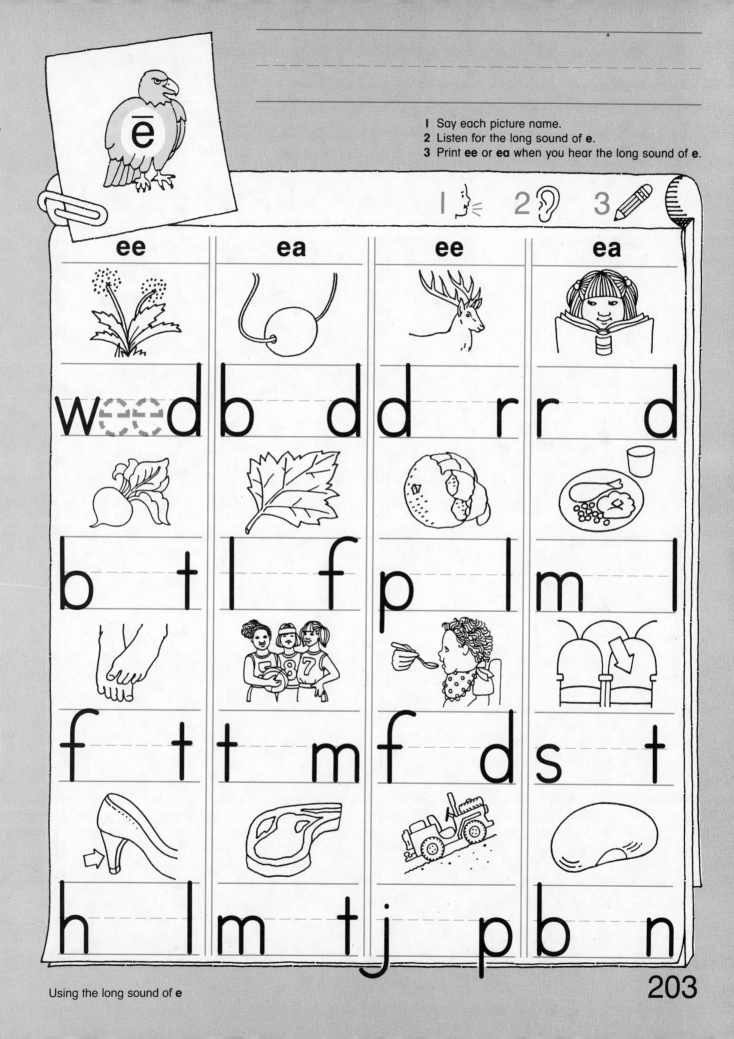

ee　　　　ea　　　　ee　　　　ea

w e e d b　　d b　　d d　　r r　　d

b　t l　　l f p　　l m　l

f　t t　　m f　　d s　t

h　l m　t j　　p b　n

I Say each picture name.
2 Listen for the long sound of **e**.
3 Print **ee** or **ea** when you hear the long sound of **e**.

I 2 3

Using the long sound of **e**

203

I Say each picture name.   2 Listen to the sound of each letter.
3 Print the word for the picture name. The letters in dark print show how to spell the long sound of **e** in each column.

1   2   3

ee   **ea**   **ee**   **ea**

bee

Using the long sound of **e**; spelling words

ē

1 Say the two picture names in each box.
2 Listen to how they rhyme.
3 Print the picture names in the crossword puzzle.

1 🗣 2 👂 3 ✏

feed seat meat feet seal beet weed meal

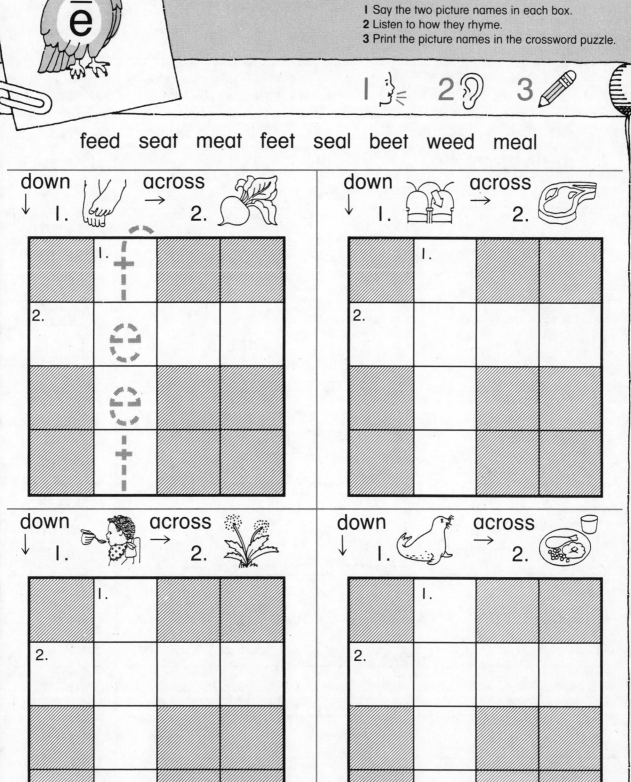

down ↓   1.   across →   2.

down ↓   1.   across →   2.

down ↓   1.   across →   2.

down ↓   1.   across →   2.

Using the long sound of **e**; writing rhyming words

205

1 Read each sentence.
2 Fill in the space beside the word that makes sense in the sentence.
3 Print the word on the line.

1 📖 2 ✏️ 3 ✏️

I can dive into deep .
○ deer
● deep
○ deed

Where is the bag of _____ ?
○ seem
○ seen
○ seed

My ⚾ team will _____ them.
○ beat
○ bead
○ bed

Will you _____ this 📖 to me?
○ red
○ reap
○ read

Jean will go this _____ .
○ week
○ weed
○ wed

The deer can _____ over the 🚧 .
○ leap
○ leak
○ leaf

Mike will _____ his dog in the 🍳 .
○ fed
○ feet
○ feed

Mom will pile the 🍁 in a _____ .
○ heat
○ heap
○ heal

206

Language arts applications: using sentence context to select words with the long sound of **e**

I Read each sentence.
2 Print the sentence that tells about the picture.

A beet fell by a bed.
A bead fell on a bed.

A seal is on the seat.
A seal eats by the seat.

Dean has meat with his meal.
Joan has peas to eat.

That deer ate a leaf.
That deer can leap on a seat.

Ted can see the seal.
Ted can wave at the sea.

1 Read the story below. 2 Say each word.
3 Listen carefully for the long sound of **e**.
4 Draw a line under each word with the
   long sound of **e**.

A queen named Bea sat under a tree.
A leaf fell at her feet. She looked up
to see three deer.

"I did not hear you come," she said.
"Please do not leave. I want you to eat with me."

The queen ate seeds, peas, beans, and meat.
But the deer did not eat.

The queen was mad. She said, "If you
do not like all these, then you must eat weeds."
And so the deer got to eat what they liked.

208

Language arts applications: reading a story with words with the long sound of **e**

1 Read the story once more.
2 Then read the questions below.
3 Fill in the space by the correct answer.

1. Is the queen named Bess? ○ yes ● no

2. Were there three deer? ○ yes ○ no

3. Did the queen eat peas? ○ yes ○ no

4. Did the deer eat what the queen ate? ○ yes ○ no

5. Did the deer like the queen? ○ yes ○ no

6. Which is the better name for the story? ○ Queen Bea and the Deer ○ Queen Bea Eats Peas

1 Make up three sentences. Use words from boxes A, B, and C.
2 Print your sentences on the lines below.

Box A	Box B	Box C
A queen	ate	meat.
The deer	like	weeds.

1. A queen

2.

3.

ā ē̄ ī ō ū

Directions: Say the name of the picture. Listen to the sound. Fill in the space next to the word that names the picture.

Examples

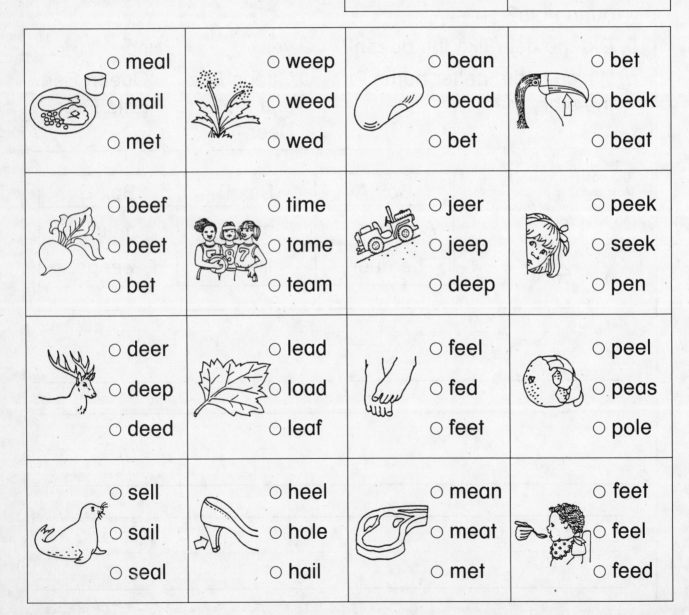

○ bell	○ bed
○ bee	○ bean
○ bean	○ bead

○ meal ○ mail ○ met	○ weep ○ weed ○ wed	○ bean ○ bead ○ bet	○ bet ○ beak ○ beat
○ beef ○ beet ○ bet	○ time ○ tame ○ team	○ jeer ○ jeep ○ deep	○ peek ○ seek ○ pen
○ deer ○ deep ○ deed	○ lead ○ load ○ leaf	○ feel ○ fed ○ feet	○ peel ○ peas ○ pole
○ sell ○ sail ○ seal	○ heel ○ hole ○ hail	○ mean ○ meat ○ met	○ feet ○ feel ○ feed

Testing the long sound of **e**; using an adapted standardized test format

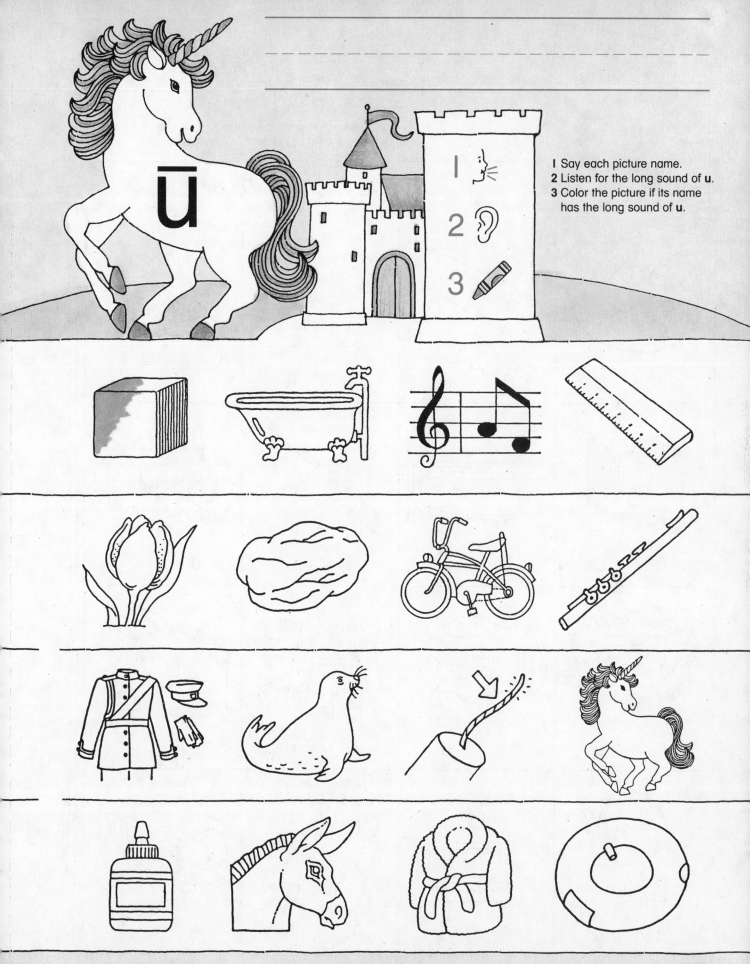

1 Say each picture name.
2 Listen for the long sound of **u**.
3 Color the picture if its name has the long sound of **u**.

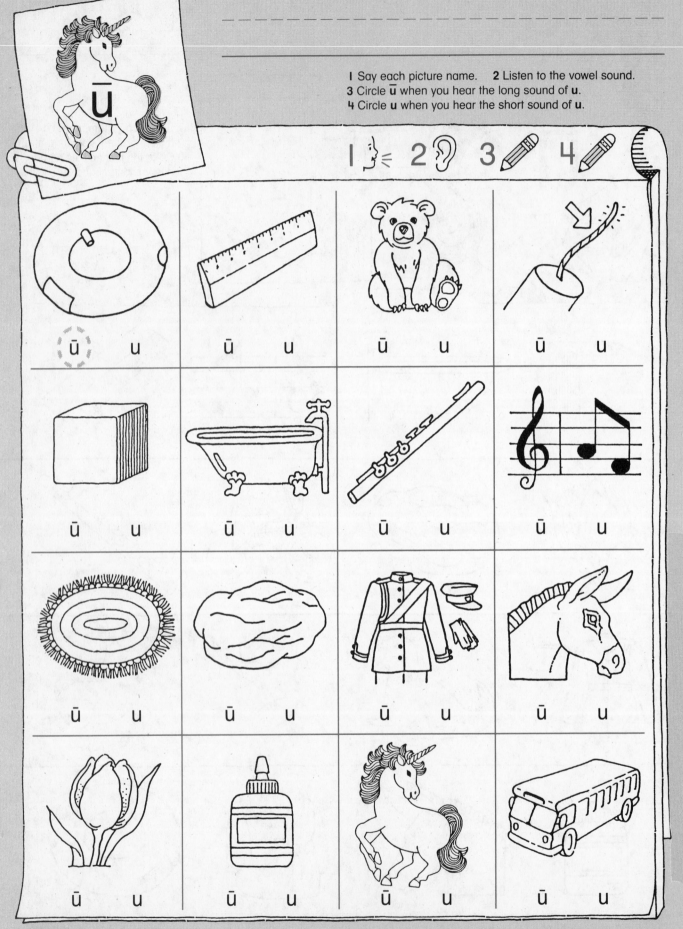

1 Say each picture name. 2 Listen to the vowel sound.
3 Circle ū when you hear the long sound of u.
4 Circle u when you hear the short sound of u.

212

1 Say each picture name.
2 Listen to the vowel sound.
3 Circle and then print the word for the picture name.

ū

1 2 3

cub + e = cūbe

cub (cube)	fuss fuse	us use	den dune
cube			

tub tube	cut cute	cub cube	fuss fuse

cut cute	tub tube	mull mule	hug huge

Using the long sound of **u**; spelling words

213

1 Say each picture name. 2 Listen for the long and short sounds of **u**.
3 Circle the word for the picture name.
4 If the word has the long sound of **u**, mark the silent letter as shown.

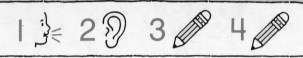

ū_e

(mūle̸) mole mud

fuss fun fuse

cube cut cute

fine fuss fuse

dune dug dine

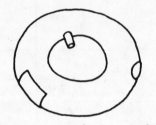

tape tub tube

mutt mule mud

tub tube tug

cube cub cute

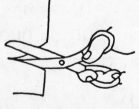

coat cut cute

hug hut heap

cub cube cape

214

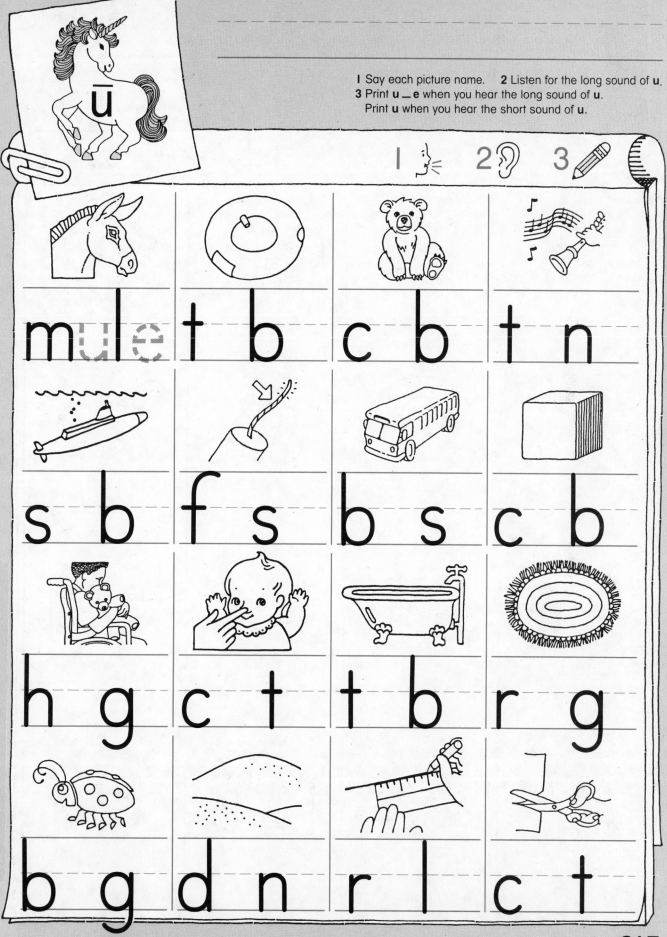

1 Say each picture name.   2 Listen for the long sound of **u**.
3 Print **u __ e** when you hear the long sound of **u**.
Print **u** when you hear the short sound of **u**.

1 2 3

mule   t b   c b   t n

s b   f s   b s   c b

h g   c t   t b   r g

b g   d   n r   l c t

Using the long sound of **u**; spelling words

ū

1 Say the two picture names in each box.
2 Listen to how they rhyme.
3 Print the picture names in the crossword puzzle.

1 🗣 2 👂 3 ✏️

tube tune mule lute cute dune cube rule

down ↓ 1.   **across** → 2.

```
      1. C
  2. U
      B
      E
```

down ↓ 1.   **across** → 2.

```
      1.
  2.
```

down ↓ 1.   **across** → 2.

```
      1.
  2.
```

down ↓ 1.   **across** → 2.

```
      1.
  2.
```

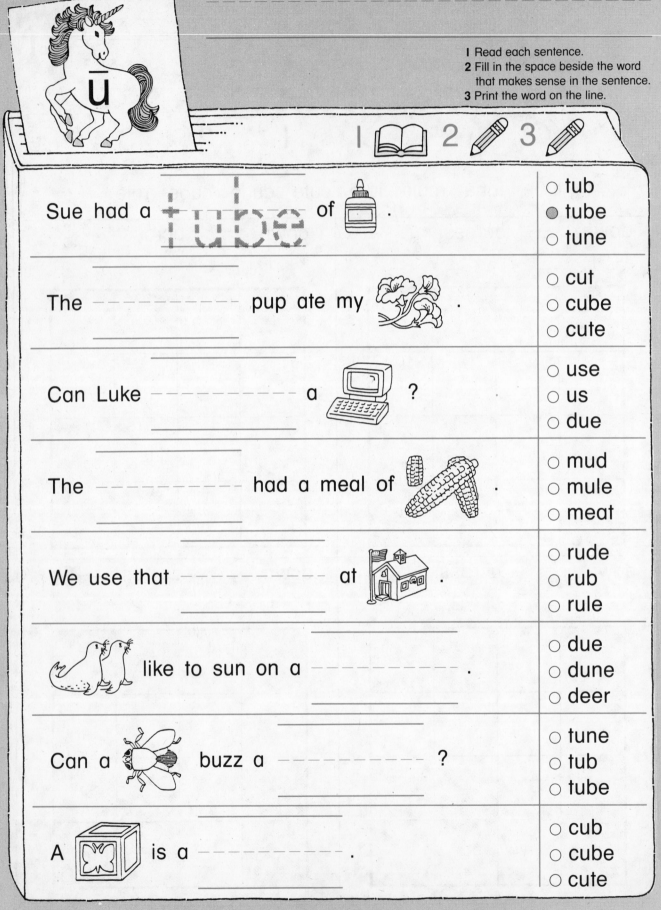

1 Read each sentence.
2 Fill in the space beside the word
   that makes sense in the sentence.
3 Print the word on the line.

1 📖 2 ✏️ 3 ✏️

Sue had a _tube_ of 🧴 .
- ○ tub
- ● tube
- ○ tune

The _____ pup ate my 🌸 .
- ○ cut
- ○ cube
- ○ cute

Can Luke _____ a 🖥️ ?
- ○ use
- ○ us
- ○ due

The _____ had a meal of 🌽 .
- ○ mud
- ○ mule
- ○ meat

We use that _____ at 🏫 .
- ○ rude
- ○ rub
- ○ rule

🦭 like to sun on a _____ .
- ○ due
- ○ dune
- ○ deer

Can a 🪰 buzz a _____ ?
- ○ tune
- ○ tub
- ○ tube

A 🧊 is a _____ .
- ○ cub
- ○ cube
- ○ cute

218   Language arts applications: using sentence context to select words with the long sound of **u**

ū

1   2

Tom gave us the tub.
Tom can use the tub.

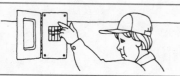
Tom can use the tub.

The cub is in the cup.
The cube is in the cup.

_____

Luke put in a fuse.
Luke put up a fuss.

_____

Sue gave a mule a hug.
Sue says the mule is rude.

_____

Jules got a red rug.
Jules gave a big hug.

_____

Language arts applications: using the long sound of **u** to select sentences from context

I Read the story below. **2** Say each word.
3 Listen carefully for the long sound of **u**.
4 Draw a line under each word with the long sound of **u**.

Jules has a mule named Luke.
Jules and Luke go to the sea for a week in June.
Jules rides Luke to the dunes.

One day, Luke will not go to the dunes.
Jules says, "Luke, you are rude. I will make a rule.
If I hum a tune, you have to go."

Jules hops on Luke and says, "Go."
Then he hums a tune.
Luke runs to the dunes in time to the tune.

220

ū

1 Read the story once more.
2 Then read the questions below.
3 Fill in the space by the correct answer.

1   2   3

1. Did Jules have a mule?   ● yes   ○ no

2. Did Jules and Luke go to the sea?   ○ yes   ○ no

3. Did Luke say Jules was rude?   ○ yes   ○ no

4. Did Luke hum a tune?   ○ yes   ○ no

5. Did Luke like the tune?   ○ yes   ○ no

6. Which is the better name for the story?   ○ Luke Hums a Tune   ○ Jules and Luke Go to the Dunes

1 Make up three sentences. Use words from boxes A, B, and C.
2 Print your sentences on the lines below.

 2

Box A	Box B	Box C
Jules	has	a mule.
Luke	can go	to the dunes.

1. Jules

2.

3.

ā ē ī ō ū

Directions: Say the name of the picture.
Listen to the sound. Fill in the space next
to the word that names the picture.

Examples

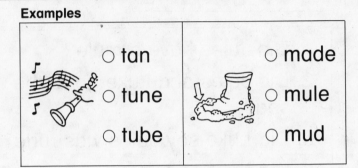

○ tan	○ made
○ tune	○ mule
○ tube	○ mud

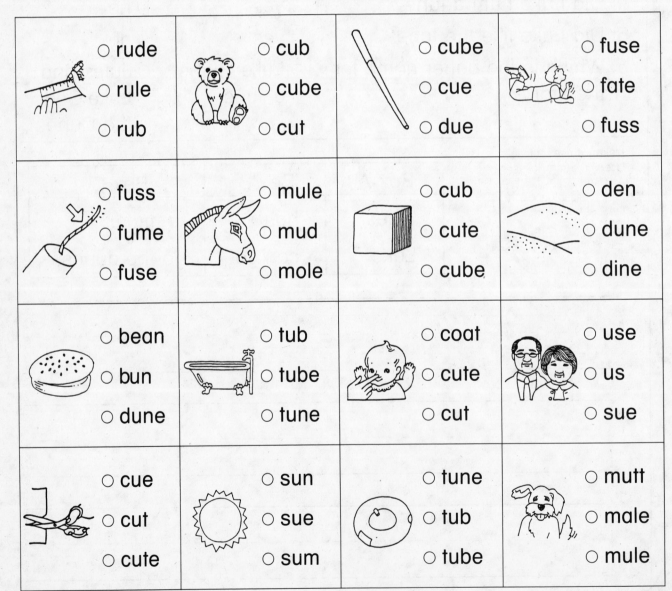

○ rude	○ cub	○ cube	○ fuse
○ rule	○ cube	○ cue	○ fate
○ rub	○ cut	○ due	○ fuss
○ fuss	○ mule	○ cub	○ den
○ fume	○ mud	○ cute	○ dune
○ fuse	○ mole	○ cube	○ dine
○ bean	○ tub	○ coat	○ use
○ bun	○ tube	○ cute	○ us
○ dune	○ tune	○ cut	○ sue
○ cue	○ sun	○ tune	○ mutt
○ cut	○ sue	○ tub	○ male
○ cute	○ sum	○ tube	○ mule

Testing the long sound of **u**; using an adapted standardized test format ā ē ī ō ū

1 Say each picture name.
2 Listen to the vowel sound.
3 Print the vowels to complete the picture name.

1 2 3

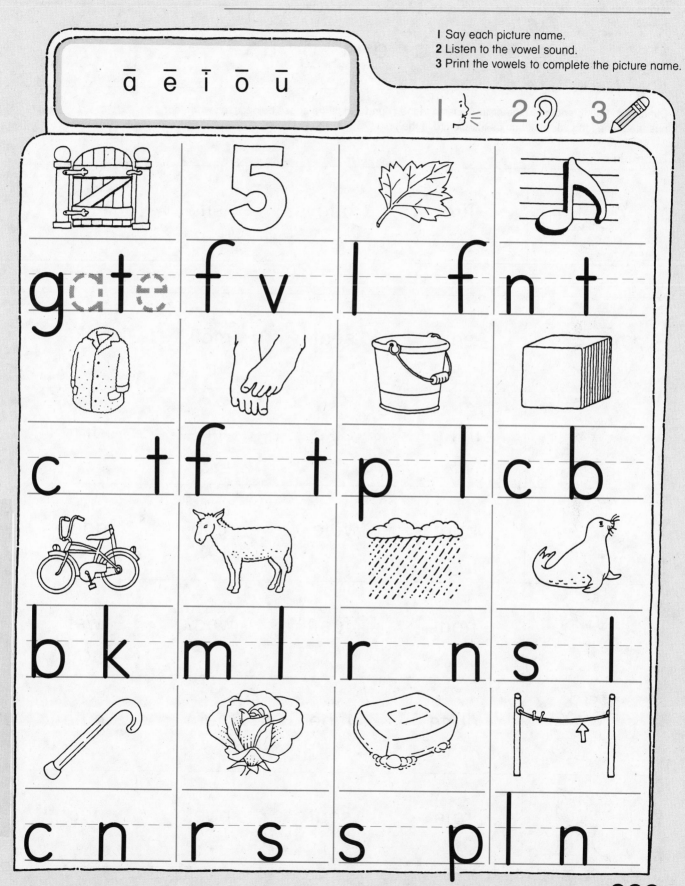

g a t e   f v l   f n t

c t f   t p   l c b

b k   m l   r n s l

c n   r s   s p   l n

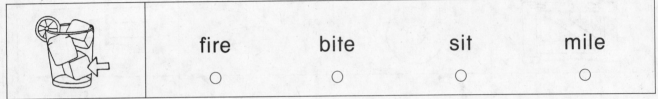

ā ē ī ō ū

Directions: Say the name of the picture. Listen to the sound. Fill in the space below each word that has the same long vowel sound as the picture in the box.

Example

	fire	bite	sit	mile
	○	○	○	○

	sail	seal	mail	bake
	○	○	○	○
	mine	bike	tire	dim
	○	○	○	○
	boat	vote	cob	goat
	○	○	○	○
	heat	feet	weak	wet
	○	○	○	○
	dune	tube	neat	cute
	○	○	○	○
	rate	seat	peek	neat
	○	○	○	○

224

Testing the long vowel sounds; using an adapted standardized test format

1 Say each picture name.
2 Listen to the blend at the beginning.
3 Color the balloon if the picture begins with the blend by the string.

225

Introducing consonant blends; **s** blends in initial position

sk sm
sn sp
st sw

1 Say each picture name.
2 Listen to the blend at the beginning.
3 Circle the letters that stand for the blend you hear at the beginning of each picture name.

sk sm (sn)

sm sn sk

sn sk sm

sn sm sk

sp st sw

st sw sp

sw sp st

sw st sp

sk sn st

sn st sk

st sk sn

st sn sk

sm sp sw

sp sw sm

sw sm sp

sw sp sm

226

1 Say each picture name.
2 Listen to the blend at the beginning.
3 Print the letters that stand for the blend you hear at the beginning of each picture name.

1 🗣 2 👂 3 ✏️

sp

Using consonant blends; spelling **s** blends in initial position

227

1 Say each picture name.
2 Listen to the blend at the beginning.
3 Print the letters that stand for the blend you hear at the beginning of each picture name.

I 2 3

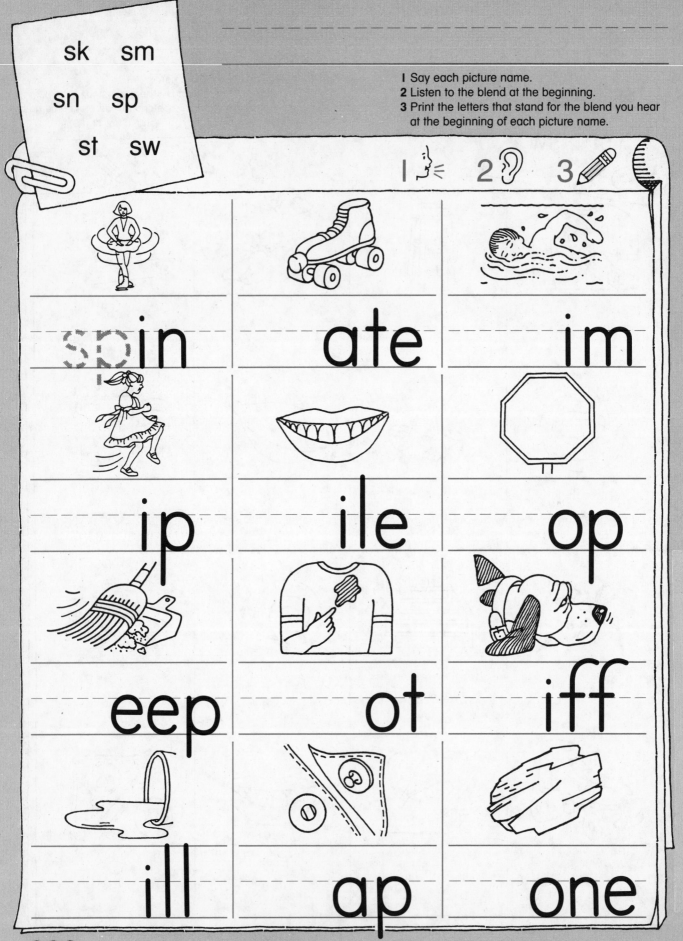

spin

ate

im

ip

ile

op

eep

ot

iff

ill

ap

one

228

Using consonant blends; spelling **s** blends in initial position

sk sm

sn sp

st sw

1 Read each sentence.
2 Fill in the space beside the word that makes sense in the sentence.
3 Print the word on the line.

1 📖 2 ✏️ 3 ✏️

Stan got eggs at the **store** .

- ○ sore
- ◉ store
- ○ snore

Do not _____ the tea.

- ○ skill
- ○ still
- ○ spill

Mom put a _____ on my cap.

- ○ slap
- ○ sap
- ○ snap

Steve will _____ in the lake.

- ○ slim
- ○ swim
- ○ skim

Did you see the _____ from the fire?

- ○ soak
- ○ spoke
- ○ smoke

I like to _____ home.

- ○ snip
- ○ skip
- ○ slip

We _____ three laps today.

- ○ slam
- ○ swam
- ○ span

Miss Dill said, "Sit _____ !"

- ○ spill
- ○ still
- ○ skill

Language arts applications: using sentence context to select words with **s** blends

229

sk   sm   sn   sp   st   sw

Directions: Say the name of the picture. Listen to the sound. Fill in the space next to the word that names the picture.

Examples

⬡	○ spot ○ top ○ stop
	○ snail ○ smile ○ nail

	○ stop ○ spot ○ spoke		○ skate ○ slate ○ state		○ store ○ stove ○ stone
	○ smile ○ smell ○ still		○ spin ○ skim ○ swim		○ snake ○ stake ○ skate
	○ spoke ○ soak ○ smoke		○ steam ○ stem ○ spin		○ spin ○ slim ○ stem
	○ slim ○ skin ○ spin		○ sleep ○ steep ○ sweep		○ spill ○ still ○ sill
	○ snap ○ slap ○ skip		○ spell ○ smell ○ swell		○ skim ○ slip ○ skip

Testing consonant blends with **s**; using an adapted standardized test format

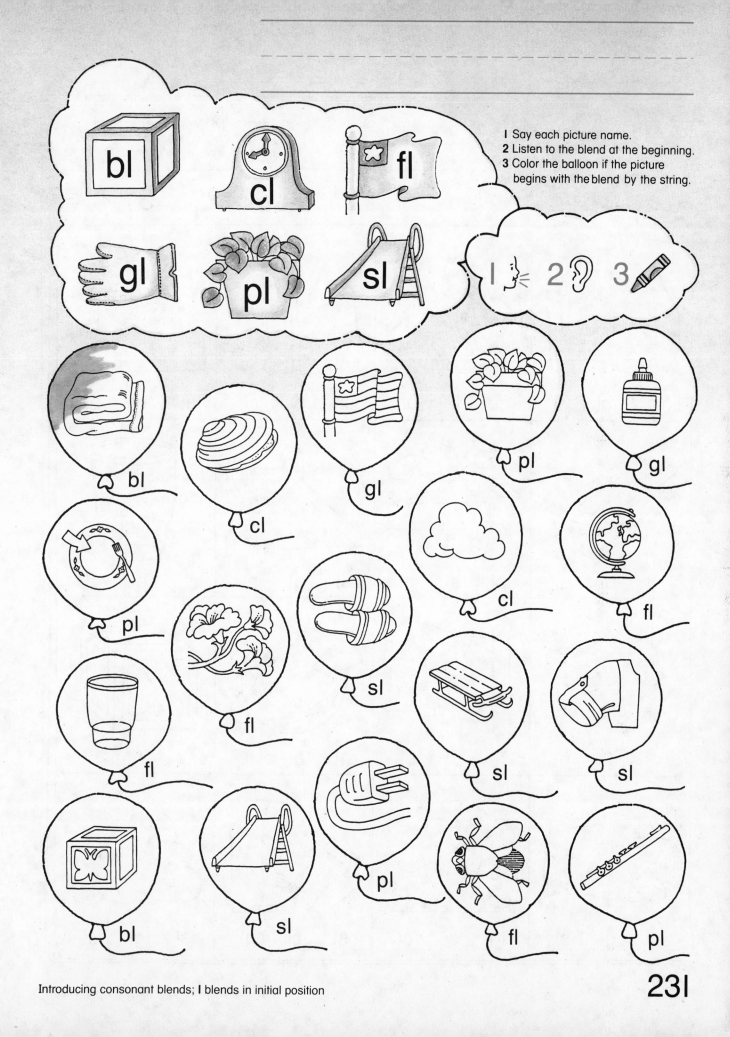

1 Say each picture name.
2 Listen to the blend at the beginning.
3 Color the balloon if the picture begins with the blend by the string.

bl   cl   fl
gl   pl   sl

1   2   3

bl
cl
gl
pl
gl
pl
fl
cl
fl
sl
fl
sl
sl
bl
sl
pl
fl
pl

bl   cl
fl   gl
pl   sl

1 Say each picture name.
2 Listen to the blend at the beginning.
3 Circle the letters that stand for the blend you hear at the beginning of each picture name.

1 🗣 2 👂 3 ✏

(bl) cl fl	cl fl bl	fl bl cl	fl cl bl
gl pl sl	pl sl gl	sl gl pl	sl pl gl
bl fl pl	fl pl bl	pl bl fl	pl fl bl
cl gl sl	gl sl cl	sl cl gl	sl gl cl

232

bl   cl

fl   gl

pl   sl

1 Say each picture name.
2 Listen to the blend at the beginning.
3 Print the letters that stand for the blend you hear at the beginning of each picture name.

1   2   3

Using consonant blends; spelling l blends in initial position

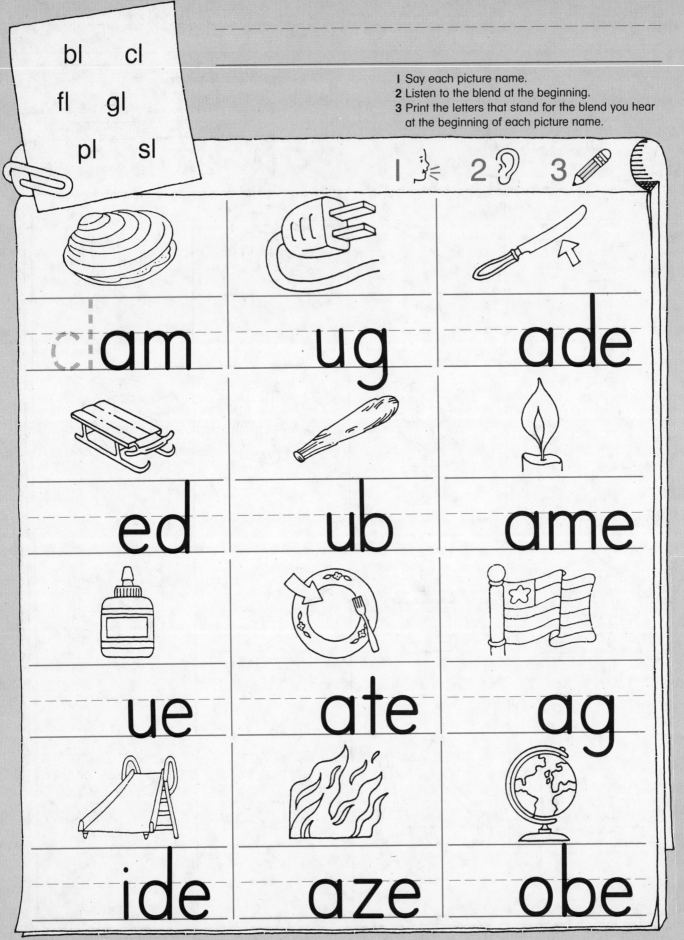

bl   cl

fl   gl

pl   sl

1 Say each picture name.
2 Listen to the blend at the beginning.
3 Print the letters that stand for the blend you hear at the beginning of each picture name.

1   2   3

cl am   ug   ade

ed   ub   ame

ue   ate   ag

ide   aze   obe

234

Using consonant blends; spelling l blends in initial position

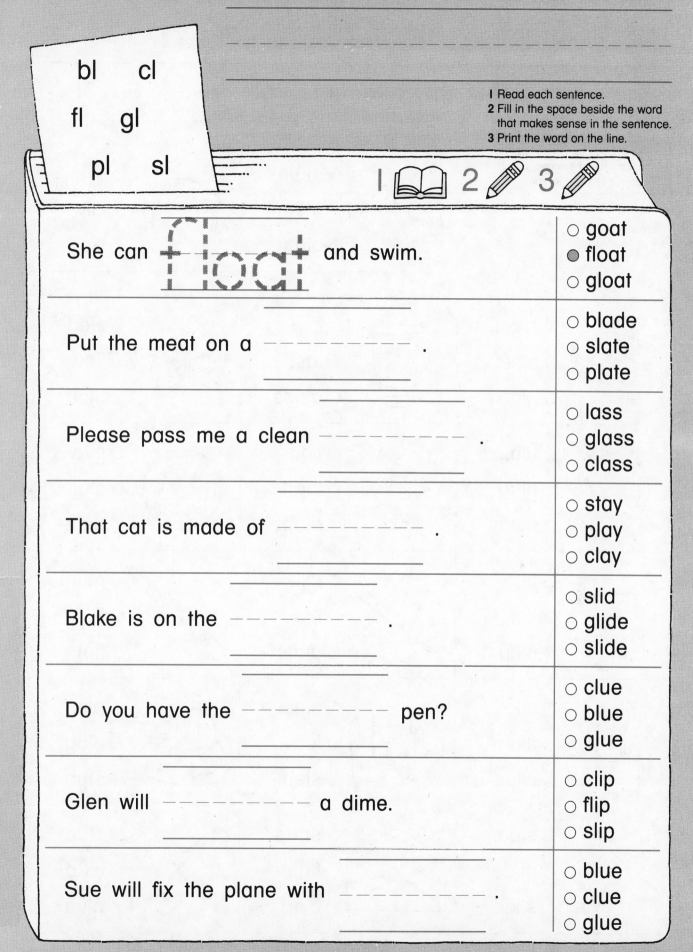

bl cl
fl gl
pl sl

1 Read each sentence.
2 Fill in the space beside the word that makes sense in the sentence.
3 Print the word on the line.

1 📖 2 ✏️ 3 ✏️

She can float and swim.
- ○ goat
- ● float
- ○ gloat

Put the meat on a _____ .
- ○ blade
- ○ slate
- ○ plate

Please pass me a clean _____ .
- ○ lass
- ○ glass
- ○ class

That cat is made of _____ .
- ○ stay
- ○ play
- ○ clay

Blake is on the _____ .
- ○ slid
- ○ glide
- ○ slide

Do you have the _____ pen?
- ○ clue
- ○ blue
- ○ glue

Glen will _____ a dime.
- ○ clip
- ○ flip
- ○ slip

Sue will fix the plane with _____ .
- ○ blue
- ○ clue
- ○ glue

Language arts applications: using sentence context to select words with l blends

235

bl cl fl gl pl sl

Directions: Say the name of the picture. Listen to the sound. Fill in the space next to the word that names the picture.

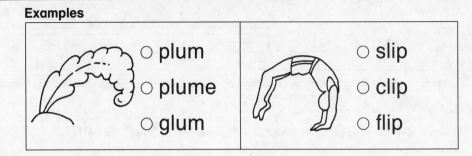

- ○ plum
- ○ plume
- ○ glum

- ○ slip
- ○ clip
- ○ flip

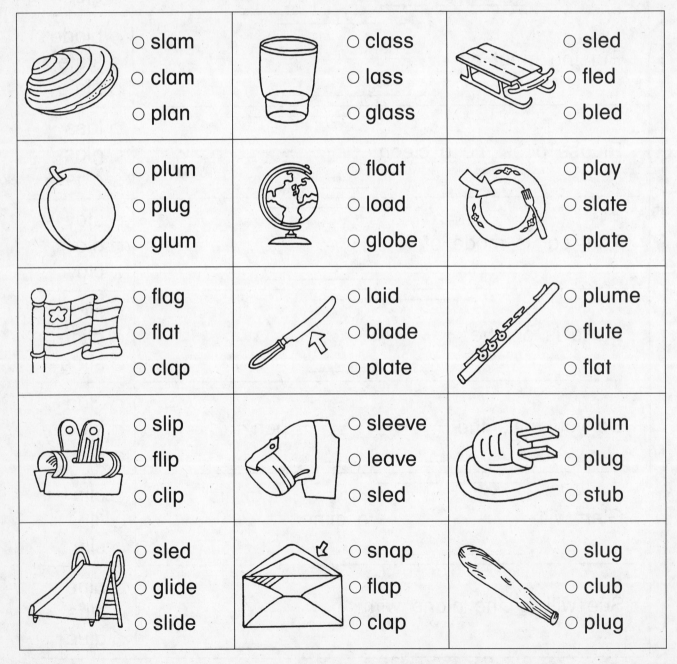

- ○ slam
- ○ clam
- ○ plan

- ○ class
- ○ lass
- ○ glass

- ○ sled
- ○ fled
- ○ bled

- ○ plum
- ○ plug
- ○ glum

- ○ float
- ○ load
- ○ globe

- ○ play
- ○ slate
- ○ plate

- ○ flag
- ○ flat
- ○ clap

- ○ laid
- ○ blade
- ○ plate

- ○ plume
- ○ flute
- ○ flat

- ○ slip
- ○ flip
- ○ clip

- ○ sleeve
- ○ leave
- ○ sled

- ○ plum
- ○ plug
- ○ stub

- ○ sled
- ○ glide
- ○ slide

- ○ snap
- ○ flap
- ○ clap

- ○ slug
- ○ club
- ○ plug

236

Testing consonant blends with l; using an adapted standardized test format

1 Say each picture name.
2 Listen to the blend at the beginning.
3 Color the ballon if the picture begins with the blend by the string.

1 2 3

br　cr
dr　fr　gr
pr　tr

1 Say each picture name.
2 Listen to the blend at the beginning.
3 Circle the letters that stand for the blend you hear at the beginning of each picture name.

1 | 2 | 3

(br)　cr　dr

cr　dr　br

dr　br　cr

cr　br　dr

fr　gr　pr

cr　pr　fr

pr　fr　gr

gr　fr　pr

tr　br　cr

dr　tr　fr

gr　pr　tr

br　tr　cr

tr　cr　dr

fr　gr　pr

tr　cr　br

dr　fr　pr

238

Using consonant blends; identifying **r** blends

br cr

dr fr gr

pr tr

1 Say each picture name.
2 Listen to the blend at the beginning.
3 Print the letters that stand for the blend you hear
   at the beginning of each picture name.

1 2 3

cr

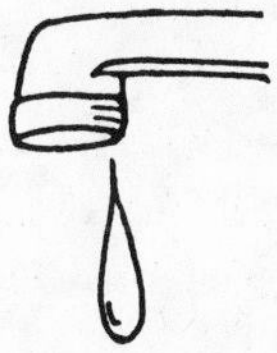

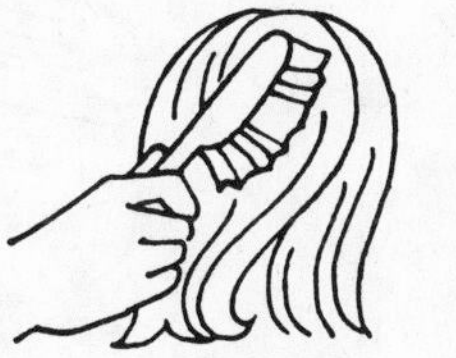

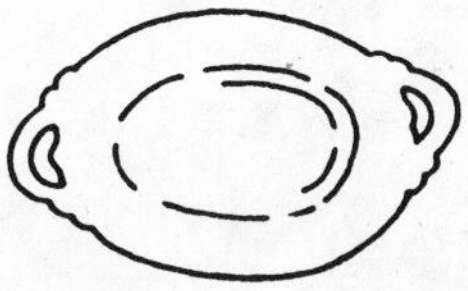

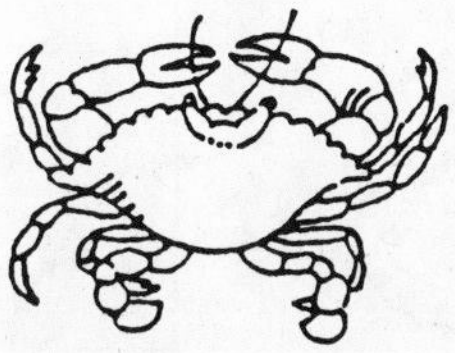

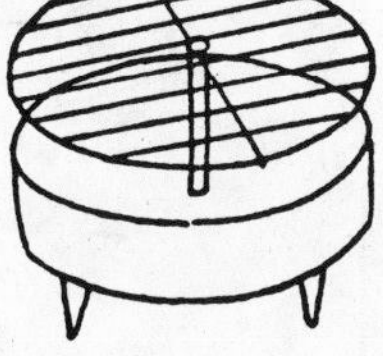

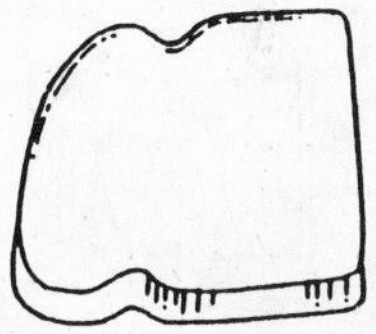

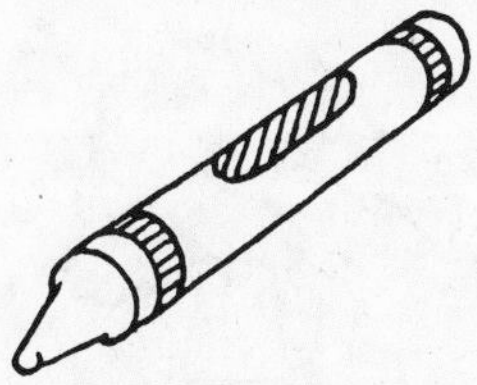

Using consonant blends; spelling **r** blends in initial position

1 Say each picture name.
2 Listen to the blend at the beginning.
3 Print the letters that stand for the blend you hear at the beginning of each picture name.

1 🗣️ 2 👂 3 ✏️

pr une

ain

ame

ane

ill

aid

um

og

ide

ee

ize

ab

Using consonant blends; spelling **r** blends in initial position

1 Read each sentence.
2 Fill in the space beside the word
  that makes sense in the sentence.
3 Print the word on the line.

1 📖 2 ✏️ 3 ✏️

A *frog* ———— can hop on a log.

- ● frog
- ○ smog
- ○ crop

Fran had a fine red ————— .

- ○ press
- ○ trees
- ○ dress

Do not jump from that ————— .

- ○ free
- ○ tree
- ○ green

Did Mom ————— a hole in the wall?

- ○ frill
- ○ grill
- ○ drill

Greg likes to eat ————— .

- ○ grapes
- ○ drapes
- ○ crates

Brad got the big ————— .

- ○ frizz
- ○ prize
- ○ pride

Put the baby in the ————— .

- ○ crib
- ○ drip
- ○ grip

Prue likes to ride on a ————— .

- ○ brain
- ○ train
- ○ drain

br cr dr fr gr pr tr

Directions: Say the name of the picture. Listen to the sound. Fill in the space next to the word that names the picture.

Examples

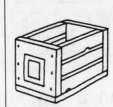 ○ brake ○ rate ○ crate	 ○ tree ○ free ○ dress

 ○ ride ○ bride ○ pride	 ○ grapes ○ drapes ○ crates	 ○ pride ○ bride ○ prize
 ○ rib ○ trip ○ crib	 ○ brain ○ train ○ stain	○ drum ○ prune ○ glum
 ○ crib ○ grab ○ crab	 ○ grass ○ brass ○ dress	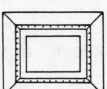 ○ drain ○ frame ○ train
 ○ true ○ drum ○ prune	○ trade ○ braid ○ bride	○ drill ○ grill ○ skill
 ○ clay ○ gray ○ tray	○ frog ○ fog ○ grab	○ drip ○ clip ○ trip

242

Testing consonant blends with **r**; using an adapted standardized test format

| sk sl sm sn st sw bl |
| cl fl gl pl cr dr fr gr tr |

1 Say each picture name.
2 Listen to the blend at the beginning.
3 Print the letters that stand for the blend you hear at the beginning of each picture name.

 sk			
	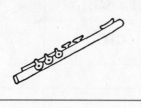		
			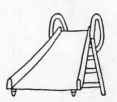

Reviewing **s**, **l**, and **r** consonant blends

sk sl sm sn st sw bl cl fl gl pl cr dr fr tr

Directions: Say the name of the picture. Listen to the sound. Fill in the space next to the word that names the picture.

Examples

○ slam
○ clam
○ crab

○ led
○ sped
○ sled

○ spot
○ stop
○ spell

○ drum
○ plum
○ trim

○ flip
○ flea
○ drip

○ clove
○ grove
○ stove

○ plate
○ glad
○ blade

○ sleeve
○ leave
○ sleep

○ frog
○ drag
○ grab

○ skill
○ still
○ skip

○ braid
○ brake
○ trade

○ clip
○ slip
○ clap

○ fizz
○ prize
○ bride

○ plum
○ blue
○ drum

○ drill
○ rip
○ drip

○ crab
○ grab
○ slab

○ rain
○ crane
○ train

244

Testing consonant blends; using an adapted standardized test format

y = y

y = ē

y = ī

1 Say each picture name.
2 Listen to the sound of **y**.
3 Color the picture blue if its name begins with the sound of **y** as in **yo-yo**.
   Color it red if it ends with the sound of **y** as in **baby**.
   Color it green if it ends with the sound of **y** as in **fly**.

1   2   3

y = y

y = ē

y = ī

1 Say each picture name.
2 Listen to the sound of **y**.
3 Circle the sound of **y** you hear.

1   2   3

ē ī y   ē ī y   ē ī y   ē ī y

ē ī y   ē ī y   ē ī y   ē ī y

ē ī y   ē ī y   ē ī y   ē ī y

ē ī y   ē ī y   ē ī y   ē ī y

246

Using the sounds of **y**; /ē/, /ī/, /y/

_____

_____

y = y
y = ē
y = ī

1 Read each sentence.
2 Circle the two words that make sense in the sentence.
3 Print the words on the lines.

1 📖 2 ✏️ 3 ✏️

Stay or the **baby** will **cry** .

| my |
| (baby) |
| (cry) |

_____

See the jet _____ in the _____ .

| sky |
| fly |
| by |

_____

I will _____ to flip this _____ .

| fry |
| try |
| penny |

_____

You can ride _____ .

| yes |
| my |
| pony |

_____

This _____ I will give Jill a _____ .

| posy |
| year |
| lady |

_____

Manny will _____ the _____ to eat.

| fry |
| yam |
| yell |

_____

A _____ day makes me _____ .

| happy |
| tummy |
| sunny |

_____

Did you hear this _____ joke _____ ?

| funny |
| yet |
| yes |

Language arts applications: using sentence context to select words with the sounds of **y**; /ē/, /ī/, /y/

247

$$y = y \qquad y = \bar{e} \qquad y = \bar{i}$$

Directions: Say the name of the picture. Listen to the sound. Fill in the space next to the word that names the picture.

Examples

○ posy
○ pony
○ puppy

○ yell
○ yak
○ yet

○ fly ○ fry ○ sly	○ pony ○ lady ○ baby	○ yell ○ yam ○ yak
○ yet ○ yes ○ yip	○ cry ○ spy ○ sky	○ puppy ○ daddy ○ peppy
○ try ○ spy ○ cry	○ fry ○ try ○ cry	○ posy ○ pony ○ bony
○ fry ○ pry ○ try	○ yell ○ yet ○ yes	○ penny ○ sunny ○ bunny
○ yam ○ yak ○ you	○ funny ○ bunny ○ penny	○ you ○ yam ○ yo-yo

248

Testing the sounds of **y**; using an adapted standardized test format

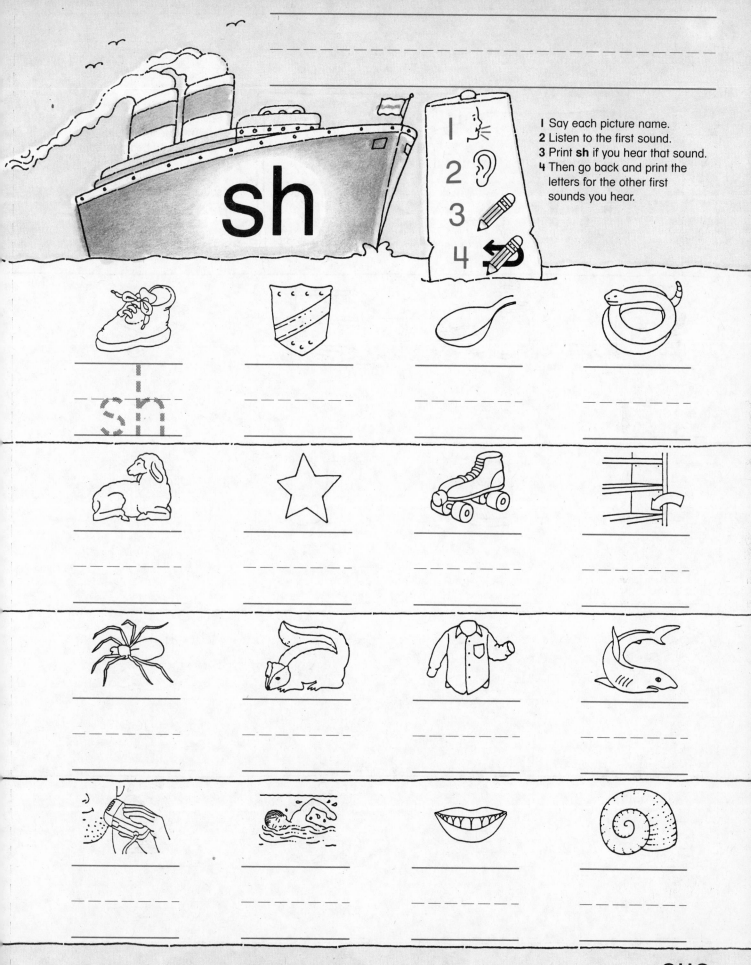

sh

1 Say each picture name.
2 Listen to the first sound.
3 Print **sh** if you hear that sound.
4 Then go back and print the letters for the other first sounds you hear.

sh

Introducing consonant digraphs; **sh** in initial position

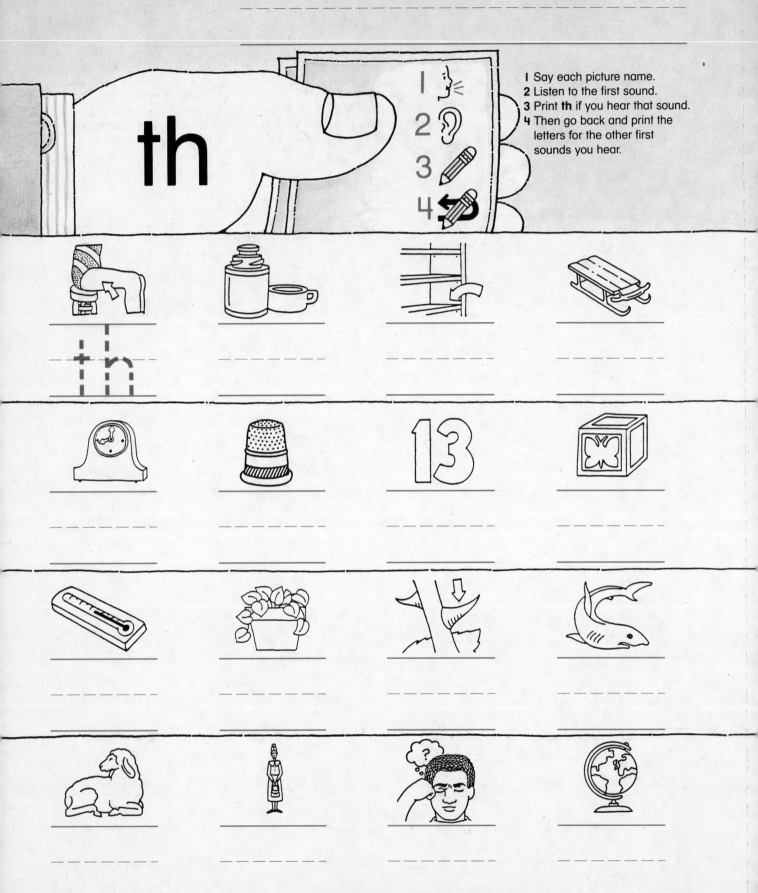

1 Say each picture name.
2 Listen to the first sound.
3 Print **th** if you hear that sound.
4 Then go back and print the letters for the other first sounds you hear.

th

Introducing consonant digraphs; **th** in initial position

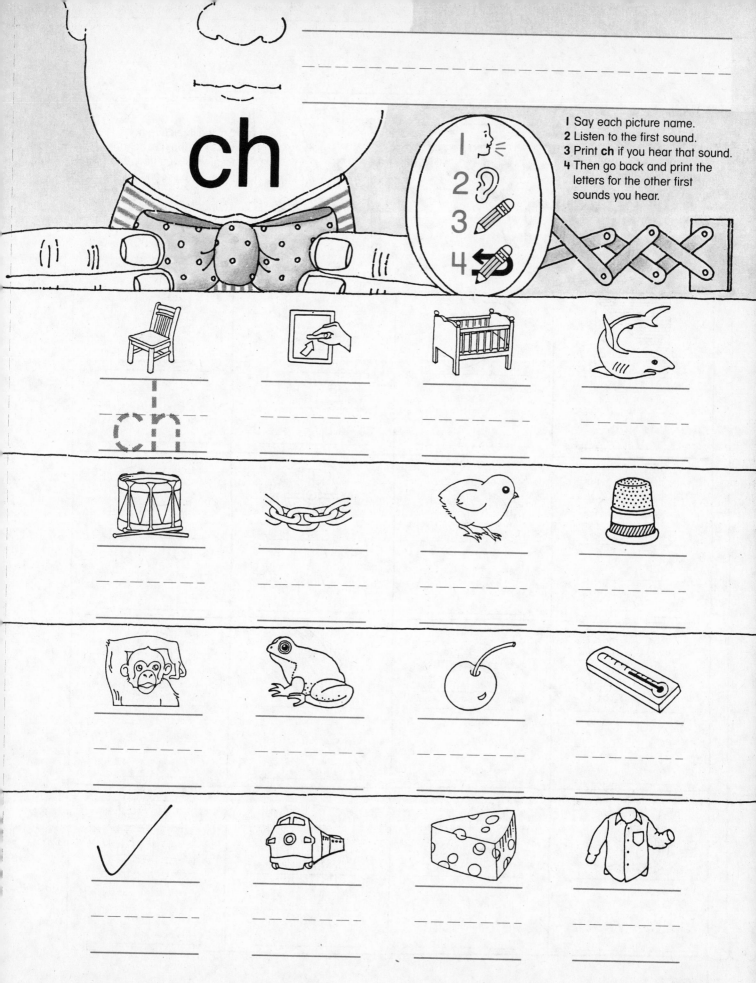

ch

1 Say each picture name.
2 Listen to the first sound.
3 Print **ch** if you hear that sound.
4 Then go back and print the letters for the other first sounds you hear.

ch

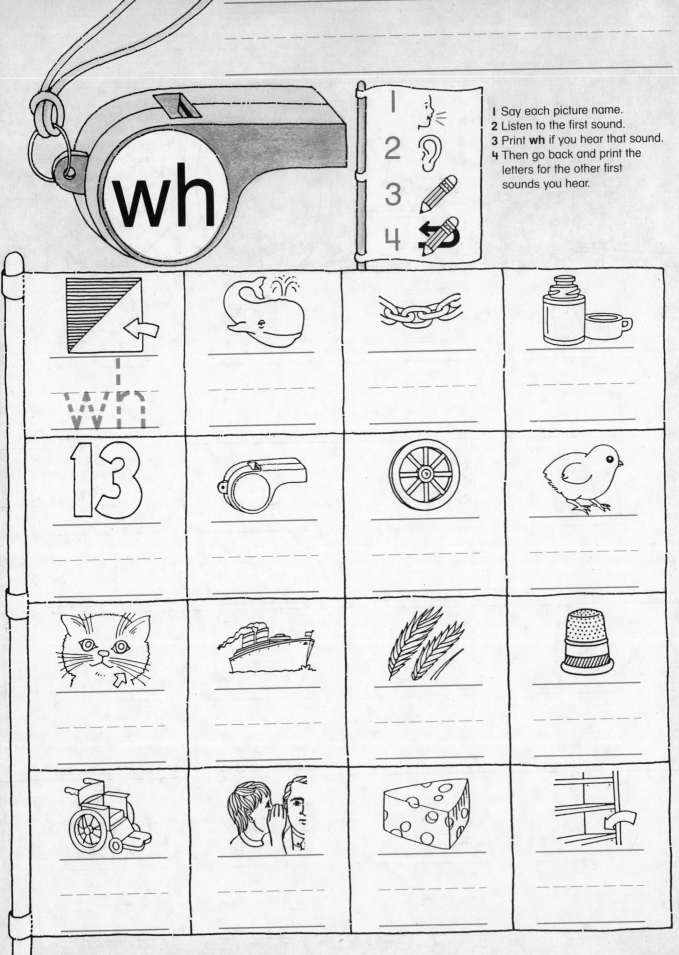

wh

1 Say each picture name.
2 Listen to the first sound.
3 Print **wh** if you hear that sound.
4 Then go back and print the letters for the other first sounds you hear.

wh

Introducing consonant digraphs; **wh** in initial position

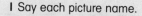

I Say each picture name.
2 Listen to the first sound.
3 Circle the letters that stand for the sound you hear at the beginning of each picture name.

ch sh th wh

I 2 3

sh (ch) th   sh wh th   sh wh th   sh ch th

sh wh th   sh wh th   sh ch th   sh ch th

sh ch th   sh wh th   ch sh th   sh ch th

wh ch th   sh ch th   sh wh th   sh ch th

Using consonant digraphs; **ch**, **sh**, **th**, **wh** in initial position

253

1 Say each picture name.
2 Listen to the last sound.
3 Circle the letters that stand for the sound you hear at the end of each picture name.

ch   sh   th

1 2 3

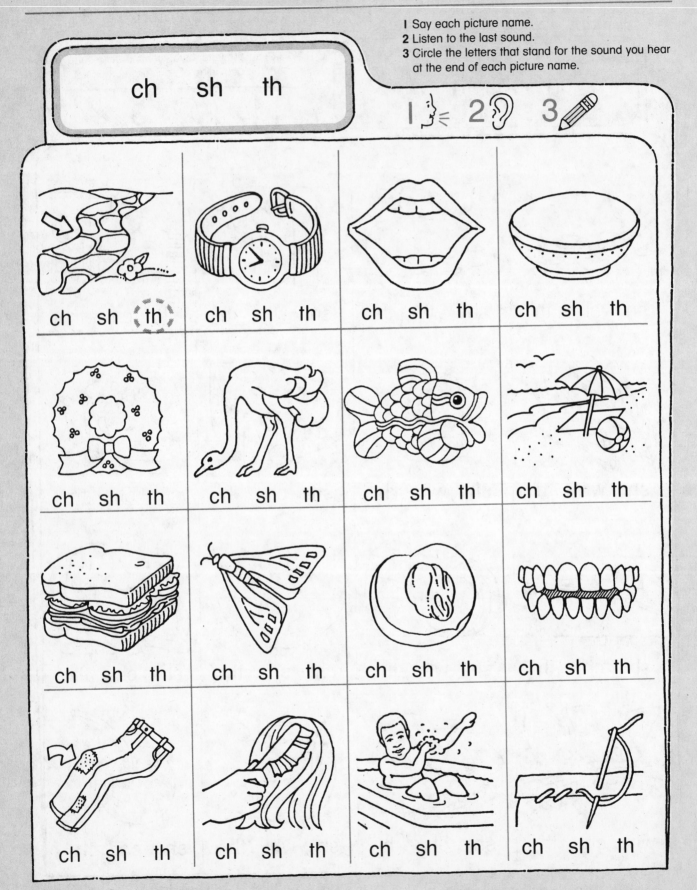

ch   sh   (th)

ch   sh   th

ch   sh   th

ch   sh   th

ch   sh   th

ch   sh   th

ch   sh   th

ch   sh   th

ch   sh   th

ch   sh   th

ch   sh   th

ch   sh   th

ch   sh   th

ch   sh   th

ch   sh   th

254

Using consonant digraphs; **ch**, **sh**, **th** in final position

1 Read each sentence.
2 Fill in the space beside the word that makes sense in the sentence.
3 Print the word on the line.

1 📖   2 ✏️   3 ✏️

The **white** goat ran up the hill.

- ○ whale
- ● white
- ○ wipe

That _____ has a big sail.

- ○ shut
- ○ shin
- ○ ship

Can you smell that green _____?

- ○ cheese
- ○ chime
- ○ chop

Shelly gave the dog a _____.

- ○ bath
- ○ bake
- ○ math

Who bit into my _____?

- ○ beach
- ○ peach
- ○ reach

Chad needs to _____ off the dust.

- ○ fish
- ○ shin
- ○ brush

Those buns are made from _____.

- ○ wheat
- ○ while
- ○ white

The coach put on a _____ coat.

- ○ then
- ○ thin
- ○ this

1 Say each picture name.
2 Listen to the first sound.
3 Print the letters that stand for the sound you hear at the beginning of each picture name.

1 2 3

256

Reviewing consonant digraphs: **ch, sh, th, wh**

ch sh th wh

Directions: Say the name of the picture. Listen to the sound. Fill in the space next to the word that names the picture.

Examples

- ○ chum
- ○ chat
- ○ shun

- ○ sheet
- ○ shell
- ○ cheap

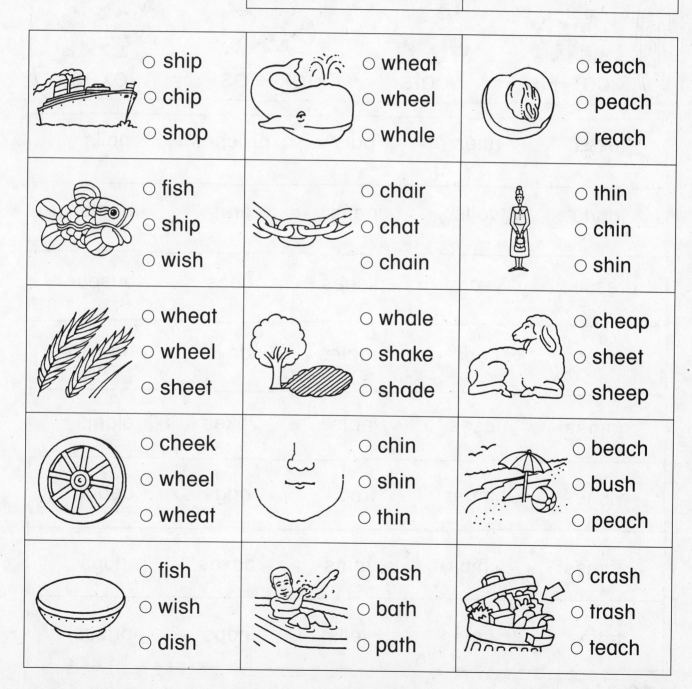

- ○ ship
- ○ chip
- ○ shop

- ○ wheat
- ○ wheel
- ○ whale

- ○ teach
- ○ peach
- ○ reach

- ○ fish
- ○ ship
- ○ wish

- ○ chair
- ○ chat
- ○ chain

- ○ thin
- ○ chin
- ○ shin

- ○ wheat
- ○ wheel
- ○ sheet

- ○ whale
- ○ shake
- ○ shade

- ○ cheap
- ○ sheet
- ○ sheep

- ○ cheek
- ○ wheel
- ○ wheat

- ○ chin
- ○ shin
- ○ thin

- ○ beach
- ○ bush
- ○ peach

- ○ fish
- ○ wish
- ○ dish

- ○ bash
- ○ bath
- ○ path

- ○ crash
- ○ trash
- ○ teach

Testing consonant digraphs; using an adapted standardized test format

257

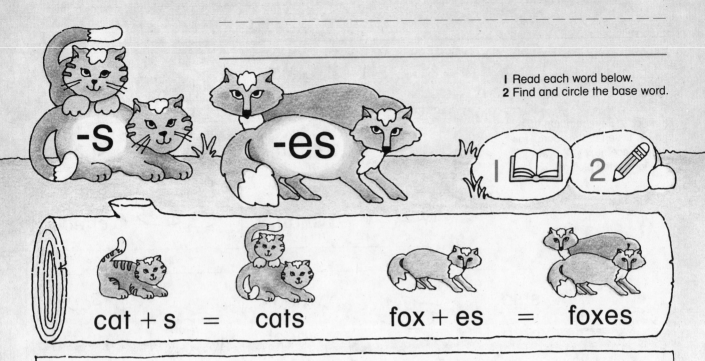

cat + s = cats   fox + es = foxes

foxes	rules	pals	brushes	pails
toads	dolls	pens	fires	boats
dresses	years	dishes	fleas	buses
trees	beds	whales	days	peaches
games	fuses	nuts	lakes	clams
wishes	homes	frogs	eggs	beads
names	chips	yams	boxes	dogs
trains	skates	yells	caps	prizes

Introducing base words with **-s**, **-es** endings

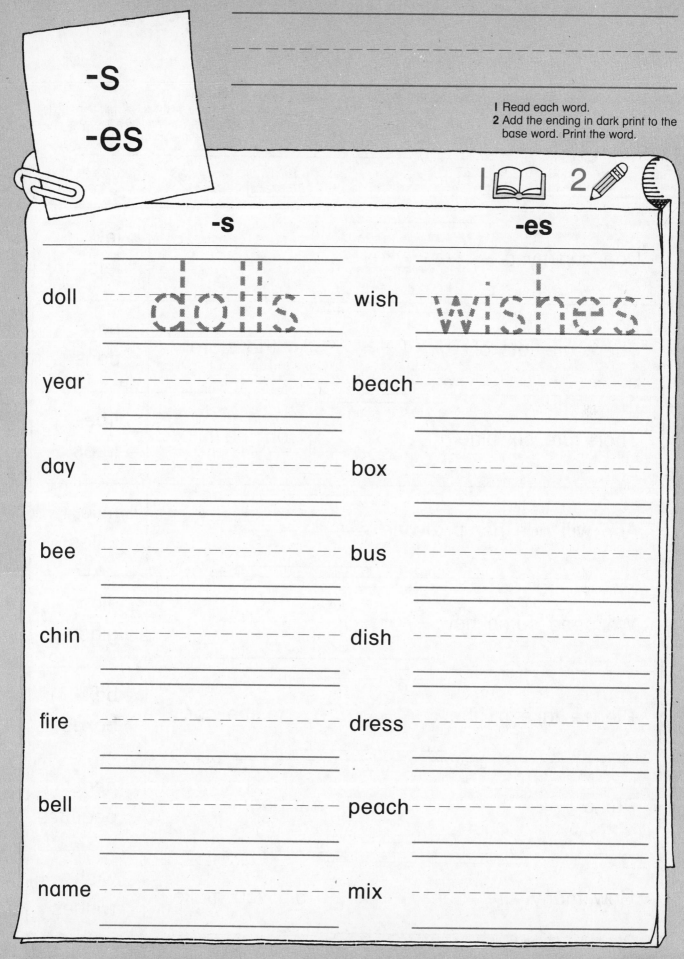

-s

-es

1 Read each word.
2 Add the ending in dark print to the base word. Print the word.

1 📖   2 ✏️

-s

-es

doll	dolls	wish	wishes
year		beach	
day		box	
bee		bus	
chin		dish	
fire		dress	
bell		peach	
name		mix	

Using base words with **-s**, **-es** endings

1 Read each sentence.
2 Fill in the space beside the word that makes sense in the sentence.
3 Print the word on the line.

1 📖 2 ✏️ 3 ✏️

Dan can fly a jet .

- ● jet
- ○ jets

There are lots of ———— in the store.

- ○ pan
- ○ pans

There are six pine ———— on the hill.

- ○ tree
- ○ trees

Ann will ride her bike one ———— .

- ○ mile
- ○ miles

We need some new ———— .

- ○ glass
- ○ glasses

Please take all the ———— to the car.

- ○ box
- ○ boxes

Put a ———— in my bag.

- ○ peach
- ○ peaches

How many ———— did you make?

- ○ wish
- ○ wishes

Language arts applications: using sentence context to select singular, plural nouns

1 Read each sentence.
2 Print the sentence that tells about the picture.

1 📖   2 ✏️

The frog is on a log.
The frogs are on a log.

The frog is on a log

The cat is sleeping.
The cats are sleeping.

A boat is sailing.
The boats are sailing.

Sally has a bead.
Sally has some beads.

That is a fine bench.
Those are fine benches.

Language arts applications: using singular and plural nouns to select sentences from context

1 Read each word below.
2 Find and circle the base word.

fill + ed = filled   fill + ing = filling

(mail)ed	pushed	missed	sailed
(mail)ing	pushing	missing	sailing
stayed	fished	croaked	spilled
staying	fishing	croaking	spilling
boxed	heated	nailed	spelled
boxing	heating	nailing	spelling
filled	dressed	pulled	wished
filling	dressing	pulling	wishing
mashed	floated	played	brushed
mashing	floating	playing	brushing

262

Introducing base words with **-ed**, **-ing** endings

-ed
-ing

1 Read each base word.
2 Add the ending in dark print to the base word.   Print the word.

1 📖 2 ✏️

-ed	-ing
clean	cleaned	cleaning
yell		
mix		
load		
play		
heat		
brush		
sail		

Using base words with **-ed**, **-ing** endings

263

-ed
-ing

1 Read each sentence.
2 Fill in the space beside the word that makes sense in the sentence.
3 Print the word on the line.

1 📖 2 ✏️ 3 ✏️

Debby _fished_ in the lake.
- ● fished
- ○ fishing

Chet is — — — — — — — with his pup.
- ○ played
- ○ playing

Shane — — — — — — — the ball to Nell.
- ○ passed
- ○ passing

Dad is — — — — — — — to the bus.
- ○ rushed
- ○ rushing

The beans — — — — — — — out of the pot.
- ○ spilled
- ○ spilling

Mom is — — — — — — — red and green.
- ○ mixed
- ○ mixing

They are — — — — — — — a hole.
- ○ drilled
- ○ drilling

Shelly — — — — — — — her red bike.
- ○ fixed
- ○ fixing

264

1 Read each sentence.
2 Print the sentence that tells about the picture.

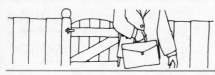

Dad closed the gate.
Dad is closing the gate.

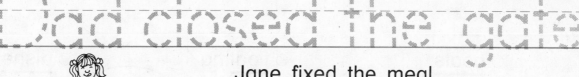

Jane fixed the meal.
Jane is fixing a meal.

The men loaded a van.
The men are loading a van.

Sue hugged the mule.
Sue is hugging the mule.

Tim spilled the beads.
Tim is spilling beads.

Language arts applications: using **-ed** and **-ing** endings to select sentences from context

-s -es -ed -ing

Directions: Fill in the space next to the word with only the base word underlined.

Examples

- ○ fish
- ○ fishes
- ○ fishes

- ○ pulled
- ○ pulled
- ○ pulled

- ○ boats
- ○ boats
- ○ boats

- ○ floating
- ○ floating
- ○ floating

- ○ dishes
- ○ dishes
- ○ dishes

- ○ brushed
- ○ brushed
- ○ brushed

- ○ spilled
- ○ spilled
- ○ spilled

- ○ sleeping
- ○ sleeping
- ○ sleeping

- ○ peaches
- ○ peaches
- ○ peaches

- ○ glasses
- ○ glasses
- ○ glasses

- ○ fished
- ○ fished
- ○ fished

- ○ trees
- ○ trees
- ○ trees

- ○ fixing
- ○ fixing
- ○ fixing

- ○ whales
- ○ whales
- ○ whales

- ○ playing
- ○ playing
- ○ playing

- ○ sailed
- ○ sailed
- ○ sailed

- ○ prizes
- ○ prizes
- ○ prizes

Testing word structure; using an adapted standardized test format